# YORK NOTES

*General Editors:* Professor A.N. Jeffares (*University of Stirling*) & Professor Suheil Bushrui (*American University of Beirut*)

## T.S. Eliot

# SELECTED POEMS

*Notes by Michael Herbert*

MA (LONDON) B LITT (OXFORD)
*Lecturer in English, University of St Andrews*

LONGMAN
YORK PRESS

YORK PRESS
Immeuble Esseily, Place Riad Solh, Beirut.

LONGMAN GROUP LIMITED
Burnt Mill,
Harlow, Essex

First published 1982
ISBN 0 582 78295 3
Printed in Hong Kong by
Wilture Enterprises (International) Ltd.

# Contents

# Part 1

# Introduction

## An outline of Eliot's life

Thomas Stearns Eliot was born in St Louis, Missouri, an inland industrial city of America, on 26 September 1888. The future poet was the youngest of the seven children of a businessman and a schoolmistress. His mother herself wrote poetry and was evidently a stimulating influence on her son, for whom she wished a literary success to compensate for her own lack of recognition. Eliot's mother also taught him to revere the example of his grandfather, a pillar of respectability whom he never knew, but whose laws of self-denial and public service became deeply ingrained in his grandson. Inheriting his grandfather's missionary zeal and sense of duty, Eliot was well-equipped to bring a message to the inhabitants of modern Western civilisation, which he saw as a moral and cultural wasteland. The habit of self-denial, however, had its unhappy side: Eliot later admitted his resulting inability to enjoy many of the pleasures of life. Often, for instance, he treats sexual matters in his poems with a disgust plainly born of guilt and dissatisfaction.

There were, of course, pleasures in Eliot's life, and his childhood seems to have been a particularly enjoyable one. As many of the happiest summers were spent on the New England coast, it is not surprising that the sea speaks powerfully through his poetry at times of innocence recalled, awakening, or revelation. Indeed, sea themes and the language of sailing are prominent in the first of his writings to be published: his contributions to the magazine of Smith Academy, his school in St Louis, when he was sixteen.

A literary magazine at Harvard University, where Eliot began his studies in 1906, printed more early efforts of the young poet. It was not until 1915, however, that the earliest pieces in *Selected Poems* were published in periodicals; though these extraordinarily original works were written mainly in 1910–11, about the time Eliot took a year off from Harvard to live in Paris and study at the Sorbonne. In these years Eliot became fascinated with those images drawn from the squalor of modern city life that were to become part of his poetic trademark. In 1914 he returned to Europe to begin brief periods of study at the Universities of Marburg and, with the outbreak of the First World War, Oxford.

The year of publication of the first four poems in *Selected Poems*, 1915, also found Eliot settling in London and marrying Vivienne Haigh-Wood. The marriage was to be a difficult one, its course marked by the nervous breakdowns of both parties and the chronic illness of Vivienne. In 1933 Eliot at last legally separated from his wife, who spent the last years of her life in a mental home, where she died in 1947. The strains of this relationship were undoubtedly reflected in Eliot's work; but care must be taken in using such biographical information to interpret the poetry. For instance, it is no use ascribing to this marriage alone the 'mad', neurotic qualities of some of the poems: 'Prufrock', which an influential editor, the poet Harold Monro (1879–1932) described as 'absolutely insane', was written years before Eliot met his wife.

After the wedding, Eliot was a schoolmaster for a year and a half before becoming a clerk in a London bank in 1917. The same year he published his first volume of poems, *Prufrock and Other Observations*, and became assistant editor of *The Egoist*, a literary journal. During the eight years he worked in the bank he continued publishing poetry and also began making his reputation as a critic, founding in 1922 (with the aid of a wealthy patron) his own literary magazine, *The Criterion*, which he edited until 1939. In 1925 he left the bank to join the publishing firm now known as Faber & Faber as a director—a job more in keeping with his role as leading man of letters, but still very much in the Eliot family tradition of regular daily work that he dutifully kept up all his days.

1927 marks two conversions in Eliot's life: he abandoned his American citizenship to become a British subject, and he was baptised into the Anglican Church. As it is Eliot's religious development that has most bearing on the poems, it will be briefly considered here. Eliot's home background was staunchly Unitarian, that is, based on a belief in God as one person, not as the orthodox Trinity of Father, Son, and Holy Ghost. As taught to Eliot, whose grandfather had founded the Unitarian church in St Louis, Unitarianism called essentially for right behaviour rather than right doctrine; it was based on what was 'done' and 'not done' rather than on ideas of good and evil; and it was concerned with enlightened common-sense morality rather than mystical spirituality. As this sort of down-to-earth, rational religion did not satisfy Eliot's more fervid and emotional side, nor his need to submit to an orthodox theological dogma, he had drifted right away from the Church by his student days. Attacks on the Church and Christianity appear in 'The Hippopotamus' (1917) and 'Mr Eliot's Sunday Morning Service' (1918), but as the 1920s passed religion increasingly offered a means of dealing with Eliot's private problems. Anglo-Catholicism, the movement within the Church of England seeking to uphold the best aspects of the ancient Roman Church, increasingly appealed to him, until, in the year that he took on the nationality of his English ancestors, he also embraced their religion.

During the previous five years he had produced only the poems that make up *The Hollow Men* (1925). Now come the last of the *Selected Poems*, with their specifically Christian themes: two of the *Ariel* poems, 'Journey of the Magi' (1927) and 'A Song for Simeon' (1928); *Ash-Wednesday* (1930); the Choruses from the Christian pageant-play, *The Rock* (1934). Even the other two *Ariel* poems in *Selected Poems*, 'Animula' (1929) and 'Marina' (1930), are essentially 'religious' poems, in that they are concerned with reverence, the soul, grace, revelation. By the end of *Selected Poems*, then, we have come a long way from the earlier satires and sordidness, though some critics have been at pains to show an overall unity in Eliot's total output, an evolving pattern of development that links these apparently opposed periods.

The later parts of Eliot's life does not concern us here, and may be even more briefly summarised. Spiritual interests, prominent in the latter half of *Selected Poems*, reappear in Eliot's five poetic dramas, beginning with *Murder in the Cathedral* (1935), and the poems of religious meditation that grew into *Four Quartets* (1943). In 1948, the year he turned sixty, Eliot received the Order of Merit and the Nobel Prize for Literature. This public reward was followed by a private one in 1957, when his second marriage finally brought great personal happiness in the eight years before his death in London on 4 January 1965.

# An approach to Eliot's poetry

Eliot's is probably the leading name in the 'Modern Movement' that brought about a revolution in English literature between about 1910 and 1930—roughly the period covered by *Selected Poems*. With Ezra Pound (1885–1972), a fellow American who championed the work of Eliot and many other experimental writers, Eliot launched a new type of poetry in English that effectively broke away from the poetic tradition of the previous age. This, established by the Romantic poets of the nineteenth century, was still being followed by the two Americans' English contemporaries—the 'Georgians'—whom they regarded as merely conventional users of worn-out poetic subjects (chiefly pastoral) and methods. Similar revolutions occurred at about the same time in all the arts, as the 'Modernists' demolished all received definitions of what art is: witness, for example, the prose writings of James Joyce (1882–1941), the paintings of Pablo Picasso (1881–1973), the music of Igor Stravinsky (1882–1971). How lasting the influence of such innovators will be cannot be assessed yet; it suffices that they all contrived to 'Make it New', in Pound's famous phrase.

Eliot was making it new before he met Pound, but his poetic practice agreed with Poundian principles, notably that the poetry of the new age should be 'harder and saner . . . austere, direct, free from emotional slither'; that it should create new rhythms and images but express these in the language of living speech (Eliot's style, though frequently 'literary', is often conversational); that it should aim at concentration and the exact word rather than vague effusiveness; and that it should tackle any subject the poet found relevant to his own experience, no matter how allegedly 'unpoetic' by traditional standards of taste. Indeed, during those two 'golden' decades of Modernism, educated literary taste itself changed, a change in which Eliot's own criticism played a large part: a 'difficult' and 'unmusical' poet such as John Donne (1572-1631) could be favourably contrasted with Edmund Spenser (c.1552-99) or John Milton (1608-74); Gerard Manley Hopkins (1844-89), for all his 'eccentricity', could be regarded as a greater Victorian poet than Alfred, Lord Tennyson (1809-92). It must have seemed to many hostile readers that oddity and obscurity were necessary ingredients if any poetry was to be appreciated by the new formers of taste.

*Oddity*

*Obscurity*

Oddity and obscurity, certainly the two linked characteristics that shocked and puzzled Eliot's first readers, are still the chief hindrances for newcomers to his poetry. Eliot seems odd or strange in both style and subject matter to those whose idea of poetry is derived from, say, a Romantic poet such as Wordsworth (1770-1850). Just as Wordsworth, reacting against eighteenth-century ideas of literary decorum, introduced beggars or village idiots into his verse and was attacked for it, so Eliot in his turn was castigated for his 'dirty gutters' or 'cigarettes'. Just as Wordsworth tried to describe every-day events in every-day language, so Eliot is not afraid to use language and situations so ordinary that many readers miss the special, extraordinary effects he creates:

I grow old . . . I grown old . . .
I shall wear the bottoms of my trousers rolled.

*comic + tragic*

That is both comic and tragic, both touchingly pitiful (pathos) and deliberately falling, in an anti-climax, from the serious to the ridiculous (bathos). Such combinations make it difficult for the reader to know how to react. Should we laugh or cry, or both, or what? Eliot himself keeps well hidden behind his highly-cultivated ironic tone, by which he can appear to be doing one thing (perhaps serious) and yet can undermine it by a hint of something else (perhaps humorous) in the words he chooses, or present a character in two opposed lights.

*modern city*

*French Symbolist*

In his joking, self-mocking irony, his modern city themes, even the construction of his verse, Eliot was influenced by certain nineteenth-century French 'Symbolist' poets; he frequently acknowledged them as the teachers to whom he went as a young man for a kind of poetry that did not exist in English. From Charles Baudelaire (1821-67), for example, Eliot said he learnt the poetical possibilities of 'the more sordid aspects of the modern metropolis', and to Jules Laforgue (1860-87) he said he owed 'more than to any one poet in any language'. Laforgue, an influential technical innovator, was a pioneer of *vers libre* —'free verse' or verse freed from conventional rigid forms, with their regular metres and rhyme schemes. But as Eliot said, 'No verse is free for the man who wants to do a good job'; and there is much freer verse than his own, which is closer to Laforgue's *vers impairs*, that is, odd or uneven verse, with varying numbers of syllables to the line, and (instead of no rhyme at all) occasional, irregularly placed rhymes. Laforgue also invented a type of dramatic monologue now known as the 'interior monologue', which Eliot used a number of times, as in the first two of his *Selected Poems* where we look into the mind of a character 'thinking aloud'. Eliot further developed such Laforguian methods as the kind of ironic 'doubling', distancing, and self-mockery we have glanced at, a cynical pessimism lightened by verbal antics, and the striking placing together of apparently unrelated phrases.

In that last category, obscurity begins to mingle with oddity. The fragmentary, apparently incoherent jumble of unconnected ideas, often stemming from the poet's compression of several concepts into a compact new image-combination, may not only look very peculiar on the page—

> For thine is
> Life is
> For thine is the

—but may also seem so obscure as to elude the understanding of even experienced readers. Sometimes, too, as with the French poets, the symbols themselves can cause difficulty: when they are not generally accepted symbols (as the Cross is a symbol referring to a whole cluster of ideas called Christianity) but ones the poet has evolved himself, the reader can have problems understanding to what concepts they refer. The value of such symbols, however, is that they can go beyond narrow reference to be widely suggestive, opening up a braod range of ideas and feelings. Whereas the Garden of Eden, for instance, is an archetypal symbol for lost innocence, gardens in Eliot's poetry can either symbolise experiences which have never been had, which have been missed rather than lost, or beauties which have to be renounced—just as their flowers are almost always among Eliot's symbols of frustrated sexual desire. Similarly, Eliot's frequent lack of a normal logical order in his poetry can go beyond a merely narrative progression to provide striking juxtapositions and powerful accumulations of suggestive images, making use of repeated words and themes and patterns in a manner closer to the sequences of music than the statement of facts in plain prose. But of course any unusual combinations of words, any omissions of expected linking phrases, any puzzling symbols make things harder for readers anxious to know 'the meaning' of a poem. Readers may not be satisfied with Eliot's advice not to bother with the meaning at first, as 'poetry can communicate before it is understood'; and that in any case there is never any one meaning of a poem as a whole, 'for the meaning is what the poem means to different sensitive readers', with their different interpretations.

Another difficulty is Eliot's notorious use of allusions and quotations. Some of these refer to well-known historical events, works of literature, and so on. Others refer to more obscure sources; and the erudite or learned nature of these can be a further problem, especially when written in foreign languages. There is no agreement among critics as to how far a knowledge of Eliot's sources is necessary for a reading of a particular poem, and how far such knowledge is irrelevant. If readers miss certain allusions, they may miss some of the point of a poem— perhaps a resonance or cross-reference, perhaps a quotation that evokes the original context as a contrast to its present context. These brief Notes cannot track down all Eliot's allusions, but even the selected allusions to which attention is drawn may cause unnecessary anxiety. The main thing is not to let your reading of the poems get bogged down in sources and references: these can be followed up later, if you are interested.

For instance, there are many references in Eliot's work to Dante (1265–1321). The great Italian meant more to him than even Shakespeare, whom he thought more varied than Dante, with a greater breadth of humanity, but not so understanding of the heights and depths, 'deeper degrees of degradation and higher degrees of exaltation'. He regarded Dante's poetry as 'the most persistent and deepest influence upon my own verse'—a comment that can be set against his remark on Laforgue quoted above: Laforgue is an early influence, Dante a lasting one. The presence of Dante in *Selected Poems* ranges from the quotation used as the epigraph or motto at the head of the first poem, through inserted English imitations of Dante such as the first line of 'Animula', to the large-scale adaptation of Dantean themes and patterns of imagery in *Ash-Wednesday*. No simple listing of allusions can properly illustrate that sort of 'borrowing', encompassing Dante's Christian beliefs, attempting the simple beauty of his language, extending the range of his symbols, recreating the whole 'feel' of his verse. But at some stage you may wish to consult his *Divine Comedy* (*Divina Commedia*), a long poem in three books, in which Dante is taken by the spirit of the Roman poet Virgil (70–19BC) on a visit to the damned in Hell (*Inferno*); the waiting sufferers in intermediate Purgatory (*Purgatorio*); and the blessed souls in Paradise (*Paradiso*). Eliot also drew on an earlier work of Dante's, his *New Life* (*Vita Nuova*), a preparation for the *Comedy* introducing the poet's love for Beatrice, in whom he sees his hope of being spiritually saved; Beatrice reappears to take over from Virgil as Dante's guide in the ascent from Purgatory to Paradise. She seems associated with Eliot's 'Lady' in *Ash-Wednesday*, developing the Dantean links with the Virgin Mary. On the other hand, in his earlier poems Eliot borrowed from Dante's *Hell*, to establish what he described as 'a relationship between the medieval inferno and modern life'.

Modern life itself has contributed to the obscurity of Eliot's poetry. In an age of rapid change that has seen the collapse of traditional beliefs about the universe and man's place in it, and the nature of man himself; an age of breakdown and disorder and tension; an age in which knowledge has increased so hugely that no one person can come to grips with more than sections of it, Eliot believed that a true poetic response to the confusion must necessarily be difficult:

> Our civilisation comprehends great variety and complexity, and this variety and complexity, playing upon a refined sensibility, must produce various and complex results. The poet must become more and more comprehensive, more allusive, more indirect, in order to force, to dislocate if necessary, language into his meaning.

That quotation comes from Eliot's essay 'The Metaphysical Poets', and it is no accident that he seemed to consider poets like Donne to be closer in spirit to himself than most other English poets of the intervening two centuries. Donne's reaction to the seventeenth century, which has been described as 'the fullest record in our literature of the disintegrating collision in a sensitive mind of the old tradition and the new learning', has similarities with Eliot's reaction to related developments in the twentieth century. Certainly the two poets share similar techniques, from their colloquial styles and vocabularies combining everyday words with unusual, 'bookish' ones, to their complex sentences mirroring complex feelings and their unexpected juxtapositions, which demand intelligence and speed of thought in their readers. Even when Eliot is critical of Donne, he could be (rather harshly) describing himself, as when he writes that the seventeenth-century world 'was filled with broken fragments of systems, and that a man like Donne merely picked up, like a magpie, various fragments of ideas as they struck his eye, and stuck them about here and there in his verse'. For Eliot's is also a fragmentary response to a fragmented age. Only late in his career, with the help of his classicism, his conservatism and his orthodox Christian belief, did he approach an inclusive, controlled vision.

Faced with Eliot's fragments, his unusual subjects and styles, his allusions and other difficulties—in short, his general oddity and obscurity—we as readers have to work at his poetry to get much out of it, rather than sitting passively letting it wash over us as can some pleasant poetry. We can aim to *accept* the oddities by making them familiar enough not to worry us by their unusualness, without losing their surprise value—one of the great pleasures Eliot can give. We can aim at making *apprehensible* the obscurities by clearing up as much of the difficulty as we can, without letting remaining puzzles stop our developing response to the poems as poetry. Only then will we be in a position to make an *assessment* of the value of this poetry for us. We may not like it at all, or like only some of it, but at least our appreciation—or lack of it—will not be based on unfamiliarity and ignorance.

# A note on the text

*Selected Poems*, a selection made by Eliot himself, was first published by Faber & Faber in 1954. The first paperback edition, published in 1961, has been reprinted regularly. Unfortunately, there is as yet no definitive edition of Eliot's poetry, by which errors in *Selected Poems* (and other volumes, none of which is totally authoritative) may be corrected. No misprints, however, are likely to be serious enough to hinder, in any radical way, a reading of any of the poems.

These Notes deal with all the poems in *Selected Poems* except *The Waste Land*, which is the subject of a separate edition in the York Notes series.

# Part 2

# Summaries
## *of* SELECTED POEMS
## BY T.S. ELIOT

## *Prufrock and Other Observations* (1917)

The dedication of this first volume of Eliot's poems records the death, in the Dardanelles campaign of the First World War, of Jean Verdenal. He was an intimate friend Eliot made during his year in Paris in 1910-11. In the quotation from Dante (*Purgatory* XXI, 133-6) the power of such friendship is described by Statius (*c*.AD45-96), one of Virgil's imitators, who stoops to touch his master's feet in homage, forgetting that they are both bodiless spirits: 'Now can you understand the measure of love that burns in me for you, so that I forget our vanity, and treat the shadows as solid things.' In contrast, the poems in this volume, from which Eliot has chosen four, present futile, sordid lives, lacking satisfying friendships.

### The Love Song of J. Alfred Prufrock

SUMMARY: The poem dramatises the state of mind of Prufrock, a tragi-comic figure of uncertain age. He is very much in the mould of the Laforguian self-mocking little man, by his own account physically unimpressive and sexually timid, cultured and sensitive. He imagines going through sordid streets to the room where the women chatter, but coming away having failed to achieve anything: though this is his 'Love Song', he cannot make a declaration of love. Nor dare he do or say anything else of any significance (his 'overwhelming question' suggests not merely a proposal of marriage, but a larger question as to the meaning of life), he is so unheroic, so self-conscious, and so shy of communicating with any of the women, whom he seems to despise as well as fear. From them he turns to a fantasy of love with mermaids until real voices call him back to the stifling real world.

COMMENTARY: Poems are not exhausted by any discussion, and this extraordinary poem seems more inexhaustible than many others, but here are some introductory points.

The title neatly undermines the romantic associations of 'Love Song' by the ridiculous name, not forgetting its self-important initial 'J.', while suggestions of prudishness may be combined with 'Proof-rock' as a punning variant of 'Touchstone'; for Prufrock is both primly proper and a test case for the reader's reactions. Incidentally, the name is not entirely whimsical: young Eliot signed himself T. Stearns Eliot; Prufrock was the name of a furniture dealer in St Louis.

As always in Eliot, the epigraph is also significant in various ways. For instance, there is the parallel of a tormented sufferer in a personal hell; the implication of the reader as a fellow-inhabitant of Prufrock's hopeless world; a suggestion that one part of Prufrock (timid and thinking) is deluding another (passionate and feeling), turning him to fraudulent fantasy rather than true engagement with life.

The 'you' of the first line seems to be the reader at first, but 'you and I' could be two aspects of Prufrock—his thinking self addressing his public personality—though the final 'we' that drowns may not be only the whole Prufrock, but a universalising touch. Elsewhere 'you' is the equivalent of 'one', or can even be addressed to one of the women, and so on.

Notice how the opening similes, likening the evening to a patient under anaesthetic and the streets to stages in a wearisome argument, and the metaphor comparing the fog to a lazing cat, tell us more about Prufrock's mental state (especially his morbidity and inertia) than the objects they are ostensibly describing. This use of images to characterise moods and feelings continues throughout: look, for example, at the coffee-spoons and cigarette-ends that sum up Prufrock's dull days, or the way he (equally pathetically) pictures himself as an insect stuck on a pin, or a crab deep in the sea. The final sea imagery of escape seems suddenly liberating after all the images of feebleness and futility that culminate in trivia about eating and dressing, but reality quickly reasserts itself, drowning Prufrock, not in the fantasy sea, but in the social world in which he flounders.

NOTES AND GLOSSARY:

The words of the epigraph (or motto), again a quotation from Dante (*Hell* XXVII, 61–6), are spoken by the most famous warrior of his day, Count Guido da Montefeltro (*d.*1298), in Hell for false advice to Pope Boniface (*d.*1303), from a flame that trembles when the damned speak: 'If I thought my reply would be to one who would ever return to the world, this flame would shake no more; but as no one ever returns alive from this depth, if what I hear is true, I answer you without fear of disgrace.'

**Michelangelo:** the great Italian sculptor and painter of grand and heroic subjects (1475–1564), a contrast to Prufrock

**And indeed there will be time:** this and the following twenty-five lines echo the words of the Old Testament preacher in Ecclesiastes 3:1–8: '. . . A time to be born, and a time to die; . . . A time to kill, and a time to heal . . .'

**works and days:** the title of a poem by the Greek writer Hesiod (eighth century BC)

**a dying fall:** Duke Orsino's description of a piece of music in Shakespeare's *Twelfth Night* I.1

**butt-ends:** ends of smoked cigarettes

**wept and fasted, wept and prayed:** a biblical imitation, in both the a-b-a-c form of the repetition (as in Psalm 118: 'Thou art my God, and I will praise thee: thou art my God, I will exalt thee') and the vocabulary (as in 2 Samuel 12:22: 'I fasted and wept')

**my head . . . brought in upon a platter:** as was the head of the prophet John the Baptist, cut off at the request of Salome as a reward for her dancing (Matthew 14:3-11)

**the eternal Footman:** apparently a personification of death, made socially suggestive, this recalls the 'Heavenly Footman' in the allegorical *Pilgrim's Progress* (1678) of John Bunyan (1628-88)

**squeezed . . . ball/To roll . . . :** recalls 'To His Coy Mistress', by Andrew Marvell (1621-78), in which the poet urges his mistress to immediate, passionate love: 'Let us roll all our strength, and all /Our sweetness, up into one ball.'

**Lazarus:** (*a*) the dead man whom Christ raised to life again (see the Bible, John 11:1-44) (*b*) the poor man sent to Heaven, whom Dives, a rich man in Hell, asks to be sent back from the dead to make the living repent (see the Bible, Luke 16:19-31)

**tell you all:** as Christ promised the Holy Ghost would 'teach you all things' (John 14:26)

**sprinkled streets:** sprinkled with sawdust, as in the Boston Eliot knew while at Harvard

**Prince Hamlet:** Shakespeare's Hamlet; like Prufrock in his self-awareness and worry about being indecisive (the line-ending echoes Hamlet's 'To be or not to be' soliloquy), but unlike him in heroic stature. Prufrock goes on (in imitation Elizabethan style) to liken himself, instead, to Polonius, the talkative, moralising old courtier in *Hamlet*; or even the court jester (the Fool)

**full of high sentence:** description of the learned and elevated talk of the Clerk in *The Canterbury Tales* of Geoffrey Chaucer (1340?-1400)

**bottoms of my trousers rolled:** turned-up trouser-ends were then becoming fashionable

**part my hair behind:** again the latest fashion
**mermaids singing:** recalls 'Teach me to hear mermaids singing', in a 'Song' by John Donne (1572–1631); as well as contrasting with the sirens of Greek legend whose singing led sailors to drown

## Portrait of a Lady

SUMMARY: An affected romantic lady is here seen through the eyes of a younger man, who quotes her words and describes her effect on him during the three visits presented in the poem's three sections. By his own poses, the narrator reveals things about himself. In each section he is satirical about her rarefied pretensions and repeated desire for friendship, which frightens him off. But finally he wonders, as he imagines her death, if he is right to feel so; if perhaps her finer feelings, though pathetic and affected, triumph over the trivia of his own life.

COMMENTARY: The title, in recalling that of *The Portrait of a Lady* (1881), a novel by Henry James (1843–1916), draws attention to Jamesian influences on Eliot at this time. Just as the situation and mannerisms in 'Prufrock' may have been partly suggested by James's story 'Crapy Cornelia' (1909), in which a self-conscious ageing bachelor visits a younger widow but never puts the 'important question' (a proposal of marriage), so the closely-related 'Portrait' is also very Jamesian, as in its use of a central consciousness (the young man) to describe the ostensible main subject (the lady); in its subtle discriminations and ironies; in its presentation of those who shrink from life; even in the mannerisms of the lady's speech—though her original was the Miss Moffat who gave elegant tea-parties for Harvard undergraduates.

The epigraph helps to focus the criticism of the narrator: the 'sin' he has committed is that he is uncommitted, though humane enough to allow doubts about his lack of involvement to creep in later. Note also the link between the somewhat callously treated deaths of abandoned 'wench' and abandoned 'lady'.

Eliot's favoured seasonal imagery distinguishes the sections: as in Prufrock's October, smoke and fog and descending darkness mark the late months of the outer sections, set against the spring flowers (lilacs and hyacinths) and sunsets of the middle section. But the sections share a musical imagery that fits in with the lady's romanticism, from the satirically-treated Chopin concert and the thin violins and distant cornets echoing the delicate conversation (while the narrator gets a drumming in his head as his own 'prelude'), through the violin and street piano serving as uneasy reminders, to the 'dying fall' of the lady's persistent music. She, ridiculed for the affectations of her drawing-room (the candles, the conversation, the clutter), repeats the word 'friend' a dozen times, clings to youth and twists the lilacs in an image of frustrated sexuality, the sadness and monotony of her life caught also in the repetition of the line about sitting and serving tea. He, on the other hand, twice wishes to escape and smoke a cigarette, and does effect an escape on the central occasion when he is embarrassed by her confession. His frequent smiles are superciliously amused, pained, disarming, self-assured, but can be wiped out by her openness; just as, though he may be going abroad (leaving the 'another country' of the epigraph) and could forget her, he imagines her memories will pursue him to worry him about his own feelings and reactions.

NOTES AND GLOSSARY:

| | |
|---|---|
| **epigraph:** | from *The Jew of Malta* (IV.1), a play by Christopher Marlowe (1564–93) |
| **Juliet:** | the ill-fated young heroine of Shakespeare's romantic tragedy, *Romeo and Juliet* —an ironic contrast with the ill-fated 'affair' of Eliot's lady and young man |
| **Preludes:** | piano pieces by the romantic Polish composer Frederic Chopin (1810–49) |
| **velleities:** | slight wishes or inclinations unlikely to prompt any action |
| **two or three:** | echoes the words of the resurrected Christ, 'Where two or three are gathered . . . there am I' (see the Bible, Matthew 18:20) |
| *cauchemar:* | (*French*) nightmare |
| **ariettes:** | light melodies |
| **take the air:** | go out into the open air, in this case to smoke |
| **bocks:** | glasses of beer |
| **my buried life:** | 'The Buried Life', a poem by Matthew Arnold (1822–88), speaks of the feelings we often suppress |
| **Achilles' heel:** | only weak, vulnerable point |
| **I take my hat:** | in order to depart |
| **comics and the sporting page:** of a newspaper | |
| **gutters:** | is shaken, like a candle-flame that may go out |
| **'dying fall':** | see notes to 'Prufrock', p.15 |

---

## Preludes

---

SUMMARY: A series of pictures of modern city life: the first two present evening and morning, stressing the smells and general sordidness of the street scene, the last two a woman and a man, both suffering inwardly from their perception of their miserable lives of squalor and routine, their respective visions of the street in the morning and evening. Finally, the poet speaks in his own person to sympathise—then everything is dismissed by a laugh; the universe is indifferent.

COMMENTARY: The title suggests a musical analogy, mood pictures on the same theme, developing by repetition and variation. The images create a general impression of squalidness (almost every noun and adjective has an unpleasant connotation), weariness and repetitiveness (mirrored by all the repeated words). As in 'Prufrock', personality becomes limited to attributes and to parts of the body such as feet and hands.

Some of the details are derived from the novels of low life in Paris by Charles-Louis Philippe (1874-1909), whose *Bubu de Montparnasse* includes the sordid morning awakening of a woman in the slums. Other suggestions are developed in a critical way from certain beliefs of the French philosopher Henri Bergson (1859-1941), including his idea of the soul being formed by the memory of images projected on to the passive mind as by a film: Eliot's own technique has been seen as 'cinematic', a series of images flashing on to the mind. Both Philippe and Bergson also influenced the following poem.

NOTES AND GLOSSARY:
**burnt-out ends of smoky days:** another cigarette image
**soul stretched tight across the skies:** compare the first 'Prufrock' image
**shades:** window-blinds
**papers from your hair:** for making the hair curl

## Rhapsody on a Windy Night

SUMMARY: Between the hours of midnight and four in the morning the narrator wanders the streets, each thing he sees by the light of the streetlamps awakening memories. Finally he reaches the every-day objects of home, which by inviting him to the routine of life make a final cruel irony, as he has just seen 'life' to be empty and unpleasant, marked by assorted unattractive sights and smells.

COMMENTARY: The title again has musical connotations, suggesting an irregular composition of a rather wild kind. But notice that the images which bring alive the poet's memory at the different times are not entirely random. Some are sinister: the prostitute with the skew eye who evokes other crooked images; the moon as a feeble-minded woman. Some are unthinking: the cat, the child, the crab. Some are decayed or dead: the geraniums (twice), the branch and broken spring, the moon again. And so on, until a mood of disorder, futility and deadness pervades everything.

NOTES AND GLOSSARY:

**lunar synthesis:** made one by moonlight

**Dissolve the floors of memory:** Bergson's idea of images pouring randomly into the memory to join together

**madman shakes a dead geranium:** a Laforguian combination

**Remark the cat . . . child's eye:** *'Le Joujou du Pauvre'*, a prose-poem by Charles Baudelaire about a poor child's toy (a rat), includes the cat eating scraps. Note Eliot's French constructions: 'Regard . . . Remark . . .'

**La lune . . . rancune:** 'The moon harbours no ill-feelings': a wittier version of a line of Laforgue's in *'Complainte de cette Bonne Lune'*; Laforgue's moon imagery has influenced Eliot's in this poem

**chestnuts . . . female smells:** also linked in *Marie Donadieu*, another novel by Philippe, whose *Bubu de Montparnasse* also provided details in this poem, such as the woman in the doorway and the awareness of smells

**Memory . . . the key:** the association of memory and a key is very common, as in Shakespeare's *Hamlet* (I.3) where Ophelia says ''Tis in my memory locked,/And you yourself shall keep the key of it'

# Poems 1920

Apart from 'Gerontion', the poems in this section are all written in regular stanzas of four lines each, with four beats to the line, and rhyming a-b-c-b (except for 'The Hippopotamus'). Eliot and Pound at this stage felt that free verse had gone too far towards looseness, and proposed as a remedy a strict form adapted from the quatrains of the French writer Théophile Gautier (1811–72) in his *Émaux et Camées* (*Enamels and Cameos*). Then Eliot moved on again to 'Gerontion', which was originally to be part of *The Waste Land*.

## Gerontion

SUMMARY: This poem again presents a state of mind: that of an old man meditating on (a) the personal loss of feeling and meaning in his own dried-up, unheroic life; and (b) the more general decay of humanity through religious and historical decadence. Despite this bleak vision, he does not totally despair: everything is not totally purposeless, nor are the inevitable cycles of nature stopped.

COMMENTARY: The title brings to mind other literary old men, as in *The Dream of Gerontius* (1866) by Cardinal Newman (1901–90), a vision of Heaven rather more optimistic than Gerontion's; but Eliot's *older Prufrock*

diminutive form makes his *little* old man deliberately pathetic, like an older Prufrock. As the epigraph taken from Shakespeare's *Measure for Measure* indicates, his voice is that of another shrinker from life, a life not fully lived. In the same speech from which the quotation comes the Duke of Vienna, disguised as a friar, advises the young Claudio (about to be executed) to 'be absolute for death' because life holds little, and old age has 'neither heat, affection, limb, nor beauty'; Gerontion lacks all these but is not 'absolute' for life or death, just hanging feebly between them.

The sections of the poem are linked in various ways, some simple— the use of repeated words like old man, dry, wind, and so on—and some more difficult to grasp. The poem is difficult chiefly because of the *fusions* it creates.

*1.* Firstly, there is a fusion of individual humans and humanity. Gerontion is an old man and any old man. Mr Silvero and the other sinister-sounding foreigners in that section are specific representatives of the general decline of religion (see below). Similarly, the international-sounding De Bailhache, Fresca, and Mrs Cammel, individual damned sinners, stand for all: ingenuity might even stretch to identifying the first sinner with fighting anger (French suggestions of axe or bailey); the second with amorous lust (as in the Fresca in the drafts of *The Waste Land* and Dante's Francesca in *Hell* V); and the third with the avarice of the rich (a camel-hair coat is a sign of wealth, and Christ said it is easier for a camel to pass through the eye of a needle than for a rich man to enter Heaven).

*2.* Secondly, there is a fusion of present and past. Gerontion's mind shifts continually between his present situation and his past memories. His very name recalls the ancient past, as does the war reference to Thermopylae; but modern events are also part of history, hence the references to present (1919) events at the end of the First World War. Gerontion also worries about the decay of religion from Christ to the present debasements, the whisper of devotion now offered to decadent gods: Mr Silvero (silver = money?) worships his valuable porcelains; Hakagawa (as in Japanese, could *haka* = tomb, *gawa* = take the side of?) worships dead artists; Madame de Tornquist (does her name suggest something torn, tattered and twisted?) is holding some kind of spiritual séance, perhaps a Black Mass (the candles as on an altar), with Fräulein von Kulp (Latin *culpa* = guilt?) apparently a guilty accomplice or client.

Thirdly, the meanings of words fuse. Allusions to past literature fuse with modernity in passages that particularly imitate the blank verse of Jacobean dramatists. The words themselves, by deliberate ambiguities, strikingly fuse Gerontion's frustration in the face of the confusions of history and the decadence of religion with his sexual frustration: for example, the passage about the frustrations of history could just as easily apply to a woman, and the whole poem is full of words that have a sexual connotation—from the warm rain for which sterile Gerontion longs, through the rented house that may be a brothel, the biblical 'knowledge' and the suggestions of vice (and the 'kept' woman and adultery in one line), to those ambiguous features of the physical universe, the shuddering Bear, the Horn, the Gulf, even the Trades (as in Shakespeare, echoes of the trade of bawd or prostitute).

By such means every significant idea in the poem dissolves into another. It is a technique that was also to be used in *The Waste Land*.

NOTES AND GLOSSARY:

**Gerontion:** (*Greek*) little old man

**epigraph:** slightly misquoted from Shakespeare's *Measure for Measure* (III.1)

**Here I am . . . for rain:** Eliot derived these first two lines almost word for word from A.C. Benson's biography, *Edward FitzGerald* (1905), together with other details in the poem such as the woman in the kitchen

**hot gates:** a direct translation of the Greek Thermopylae, a pass in Greece, the scene of a great battle with the Persians (480BC)

**the Jew squats:** the first unflattering portrayal of Jews in *Selected Poems*: there are others in the next poem, in 'A Cooking Egg' and in 'Sweeney Among the Nightingales'

**estaminet:** (*French, of Belgian origin*) small café

**stone-crop:** fleshy herb with small flowers

**merds:** (*from the French, 'merde'*) dung, excrement

**gutter:** the struggling flame of the fire

**Signs . . . wonders:** a quotation from a sermon preached by Bishop Lancelot Andrewes (1555–1626) on Christmas Day 1618 on the text Luke 2:12–14 (the Angel tells the shepherds of the birth of Christ, swaddled in a manger)

**'We would see a sign!':** the cry to Christ of the unbelievers who wanted a miracle (Matthew 12:38)

**The word . . . with darkness:** derived from the same sermon by Andrewes: 'the Word without a word; the eternal Word not able to speak a word . . . swaddled . . . with the swaddling bands of darkness' (Job 38:9). For the association of Christ and the Word, see the opening of St John's Gospel

**juvescence:** Eliot's alteration of 'juvenescence' refers through Latin to the 'joyful', 'young' time of year, spring

**Christt the tiger:** recalls 'The Tiger', a poem by William Blake (1757–1827), contrasting God's creation of this fierce beast and the gentle lamb—a more usual symbol for Christ: as Andrewes says, 'Christ is no wild-cat' (Christmas sermon of 1622)

**In depraved . . . judas:** each detail of this line comes from the opening paragraph of Chapter 18 in *The Education of Henry Adams* (1918), where Adams (1838–1918) describes the lush spring in Maryland. Eliot's selection of detail stresses the 'depravity': May is too beautiful to be good; red-blossoming dogwood could be menacing or, with the chestnut, sexual; the judas tree recalls the betrayer of Christ

**To be eaten . . . drunk:** as are Christ's body and blood in the bread and wine of Holy Communion

**Mr Silvero:** for this and other characters, see Commentary above, p.20

**Limoges:** a town in France, noted for its porcelain

**Titians:** paintings by the great Venetian artist Titian (1487?–1576)

**Vacant shuttles . . . the wind:** compresses into an image of futility the complaint of Job in the Bible that his days 'are swifter than a weaver's shuttle, and are spent without hope . . . my life is wind' (Job 7:6–7); 'The void awaits surely all them that weave the wind' is a passage appearing in the first chapter (already published) of James Joyce's famous novel *Ulysses* (1922)

**contrived corridors:** brings not only general deception and complication but also the particular Polish Corridor to mind —a strip of land taken from Germany by the Treaty of Versailles in the year (1919) Eliot wrote this poem

**wrath-bearing tree:** particularly suggests 'the tree of the knowledge of good and evil' (see the Bible, Genesis 2:17), which brought God's anger when Adam and Eve ate its forbidden fruit

**concitation:** (*from the Latin*) rousing up, excitement

**I that was near . . . therefrom:** recalls a line in *The Changeling*, a play by Thomas Middleton (1580–1627): 'I am that of your blood was taken from you' (V.3)

**inquisition:** notice the religious overtones, hinting of the Inquisition, a body set up by the Roman Catholic Church to seek out and punish heretics

**multiply . . . mirrors:** by increasing the number of images and angles seen, as Sir Epicure says in *The Alchemist*, a comedy by Ben Jonson (1572-1637): 'my glasses/Cut in more subtle angles, to disperse/And multiply the figures, as I walk/Naked between my *succubae* [concubines]'. There may also be a further link with the Hall of Mirrors in which the Treaty was signed at Versailles

**whirled . . . Bear:** the idea that the damned are carried away, after death, into space (the Great Bear is a constellation), as in the classical imagery of these lines from *Bussy D'Ambois*, a tragedy by George Chapman (1572?-1634) that Eliot gave as his source:

'. . . those that suffer/Beneath the chariot of the snowy Bear'

**fractured atoms:** the atom was first split in 1919

**Belle Isle:** a small island in the straits between Newfoundland and Labrador

**Horn:** Cape Horn, southern tip of South America

**Gulf:** Gulf Stream (ocean current)

**Trades:** trade winds

---

## Burbank with a Baedeker: Bleistein with a Cigar

SUMMARY: Decline from past to present is here portrayed in an impression of Venice, visited by contrasted tourists, the sensitive Burbank set against the second appearance of Eliot's repulsive Jews. After falling for a sexual adventuress, soft Burbank loses out to hard cash (Bleistein then Klein) and is left with his thoughts.

COMMENTARY: From the very large number of allusions (most of them to Venice) in this short poem, one can see what fun Eliot has had in taking his allusive technique so far. The guidebook in the title gives the clue, and in the epigraph we find a guidebook-type potted history of Venice in literature, mixing the serious and the trivial, the great and the decayed, the noble and the depraved. Sexual depravity is prominent in the poem, as expected in the city famed for its courtesans ('Princess' Volupine is evidently one such) and notorious in Shakespeare's day as the 'best flesh-shambles' in Italy. As for Shakespeare's Shylock, 'Merchant of Venice', he obviously assisted Eliot's presentation of the international Jewish businessmen (Sir Ferdinand Klein anticipates Sir Alfred Mond in 'A Cooking Egg') who succeed where poor cultivated Burbank does not: even the ignorant, ape-like Bleistein, with his rich man's phallic cigar, seems to have better luck than the impotent idealist.

NOTES AND GLOSSARY:

| | |
|---|---|
| **Burbank:** | Eliot may be recalling the American botanist Luther Burbank (1849–1926) |
| **Baedeker:** | a once-popular guidebook series, known for its compact entries with historical and other information for tourists |
| **Bleistein:** | German name (meaning Leadstone) of a Jewish fur-dealer in London that Eliot may have noticed there |
| **Tra . . . laire:** | adapted from the second of Gautier's 'Variations on the Carnival of Venice' in *Enamels and Cameos* (1852) |
| **nil . . . fumus:** | 'nothing but the divine lasts; the rest is smoke'— written round a smoky candle in a painting of martyred St Sebastian by Eliot's favourite artist, Andrea Mantegna (1431–1506), in Venice (Palazzo della Cà d'Oro) |
| **the gondola . . . pink:** | from the first chapter of *The Aspern Papers* (1888), a Venetian story by Henry James |
| **goats and monkeys:** | in Shakespeare's *Othello* (IV.1), the 'Moor of Venice' names traditionally lustful animals in his rage against his wife Desdemona and her supposed lover |
| **with such hair too!:** | from 'A Toccata of Galuppi's', a poem of decay and death by Robert Browning (1812–89), invoking the Venetian composer Baldassare Galuppi (1706–84) |
| **so . . . departed:** | these closing words of *The Entertainment of Alice, Dowager Countess of Derby*, by John Marston (1575?–1634), are the only ones in the epigraph without a clear connection with Venice: perhaps Eliot's joke here is to direct the reader to the Venetian play by Marston quoted in the third stanza, or even to his Venetian *The Insatiate Countess*—a more likely counterpart to the insatiable Princess Volupine |
| **a little bridge:** | perhaps a smaller 'Bridge of Sighs', over which Venetian prisoners went to execution, as Burbank to his 'fall' |
| **Descending at a small hotel:** | another obscure joke may connect Burbank with two civilised Americans, Henry Adams and Henry James, who, as Eliot had recently written (*The Athenaeum*, 23 May 1919), arrive in Europe and 'descend at the same hotel' |

**Volupine:**  this name combines the voluptuous with the wolfish (lupine) and foxy (vulpine); compare also Ben Jonson's Venetian comedy of the grasping *Volpone, or The Fox*

**They were together, and he fell:** a comic reversal of a line from 'The Sisters' ('They . . . she fell'—seduced by an earl), a poem by Alfred, Lord Tennyson

**Defunctive music:**  funeral music; a phrase used by Shakespeare in 'The Phoenix and the Turtle', for 'Love and constancy is dead' (as Burbank discovers)

**passing bell:**  rung at a person's death

**God Hercules:**  in Shakespeare's *Antony and Cleopatra* strange music shows that 'the God Hercules, whom Antony lov'd,/Now leaves him' (IV.3) because he has abandoned the military life of a soldier for the love of Cleopatra

**horses:**  which draw the chariot (hence 'axletree') of the sun, as depicted on the bronze doors of St Mark's Cathedral, Venice, or in Marston's Venetian play, *Antonio's Revenge* (I.1): 'the dapple grey coursers of the morn/Beat up the light with their bright silver hooves . . .'

**Istria:**  a peninsula east of Venice

**shuttered:**  so that her doings cannot be seen, as well as shading from the sun

**barge/Burned . . . :**  recalls Shakespeare's description in *Antony and Cleopatra* of Cleopatra's barge that 'Burn'd on the water' (II.2)

**protozoic slime:**  where the lowest forms of life began. Protozoa are microscopic animals consisting of a single cell

**Canaletto:**  a painter (1697–1768) famed for his pictures of the canals of Venice

**On the Rialto:**  a phrase used more than once by Shylock the Jew in Shakespeare's *The Merchant of Venice*, referring to the building in Venice where business deals were made. Eliot continues the traditional associations of Jews with money (and the fur trade in the following lines)

**phthisic:**  wasted by consumptive disease

**Lights, lights:**  twice in Shakespeare (*Hamlet* III.2; *Othello* I.1) lights are called for on occasions of apparent treachery and sexual misdemeanour; hence the relevance to Princess Volupine's infidelity

**Klein:**  literally 'small' (another German name)

**clipped the lion's wings . . . :** a winged lion is the emblem of St Mark and Venice. A link with 'Time's ruins' is suggested by a line by Jonathan Swift (1667–1745) in the introduction to *A Tale of a Tub*, where hack writers who have 'clipped his wings, pared his nails, filed his teeth' triumph over Time; see also the opening of Shakespeare's Sonnet 19: 'Devouring Time, blunt thou the lion's paws'

**meditating . . . ruins:** recalls 'To meditate amongst decay, and stand / A ruin amidst ruins', from *Childe Harold's Pilgrimage* (IV, xxv) by Lord Byron (1788–1824), concluding Byron's lament for once-great Venice

**seven laws:** presumably the seven principles of architecture of John Ruskin (1819–1900), whose *The Stones of Venice* describes the decline of Venetian Gothic architecture

---

## Sweeney Erect

---

SUMMARY: A grandly inflated opening, with classical references to desertions in the heroic past, degenerates into a sordid modern affair in a brothel ('the ladies of the corridor' and 'the house' seem euphemistic), with Sweeney callously shaving while the woman left in the bed, a nameless epileptic, has a fit. The madam, Mrs Turner, and her 'ladies', are indignant for their reputation; but one sensibly brings restoratives.

COMMENTARY: The caricature Jew of the two previous poems is now replaced by the caricature Irishman, and a stagey exaggeration marks the poem from the deliberately overwrought classical setting to the grotesque modern contrast in the horrid portrayal of Sweeney and the unfortunate woman whose epilepsy parallels a violent sexual encounter with an ape-man. He, despite the sinister razor, seems milder after he has pompously (and mock-Emersonianly) 'addressed' himself to shave, all fat and pink and unconcerned, a would-be man-of-the-world who thinks he understands women; and the tone changes to fit the lighter satire on the selfish concern of Mrs Turner and her ladies, till the 'But' suggests some praise for practical Doris at least.

NOTES AND GLOSSARY:

**Sweeney:** recalls Sweeney Todd, the demon barber of Soho who, as created in the 1840s for a melodrama (though reputedly based on fact) by T.P. Prest, cut his victims' throats while shaving them. Eliot seems to have based his character on an Irishman who taught him boxing at Harvard

| | |
|---|---|
| **Erect:** | this humorously combines a sexual significance with a human definition of the apelike Sweeney as *homo erectus*, upright man—earlier than *homo sapiens*, modern 'wise' man. It also hints at an ironic reversal of the view of man held by Ralph Waldo Emerson (1803-82), as in his essay 'Self-Reliance', where independent man 'stands in the erect position . . . works miracles'—a view that Eliot's portrayal of Sweeney will undermine |
| **epigraph:** | from *The Maid's Tragedy* (II.ii) by Francis Beaumont (1584-1616) and John Fletcher (1579-1625): the broken-hearted Aspatia, who has lost Amintor, tells her maids to model their needlework picture of Ariadne, who lost Theseus, on herself, and to make the background appropriately miserable. The poem then takes up these instructions |
| **unstilled Cyclades:** | ring of Greek islands in the Aegean, subject to winds and earthquakes (with new islands appearing, as in 1570 and 1770) |
| **anfractuous:** | twisting, winding, contorted |
| **Aeolus:** | Greek god of winds |
| **Ariadne:** | in Greek myth, this daughter of King Minos of Crete loved the Athenian Theseus and gave him string to help him get out of the Cretan labyrinth, into which he went to kill the Minotaur, her monstrous half-brother; but later Theseus abandoned her on the Cycladic island of Naxos |
| **perjured sails:** | if he successfully killed the Minotaur, Theseus was to change the black sails with which he set out; but he forgot, and his father, Aegeus, misled by the 'lying' sails, threw himself into the sea that was then named after him |
| **Nausicaa:** | in the *Odyssey* of Homer, the ancient and perhaps mythical Greek epic poet, this princess helps Odysseus the morning after he is shipwrecked on her island; though eager for marriage to him, but not wishing to appear a man-hunter, she and her father, Alcinous, remove all obstacles to his return home |
| **Polypheme:** | Odysseus escapes from the cave of man-eating Polyphemus, leader of a race of one-eyed giants, the Cyclopes, by blinding him while he slept, and hiding away among the sheep let out in the morning to graze |

**orang-outang:**      apeman Sweeney will later also suggest 'The Murders in the Rue Morgue', a story by Edgar Allan Poe (1809–49) in which the murders occur after an orang-outang takes its master's razor, lathers its own face in front of a looking-glass, and attempts to shave

**root of knots:**      another reversal of Emerson, who in his essay 'History' grandly calls man 'a knot of roots, whose flower and fruitage is the world'—a superior being quite unlike Eliot's monstrous creation

**The lengthened . . . said Emerson:** in 'Self-Reliance', Emerson states that 'An institution is the lengthened shadow of one man . . . and all history resolves itself very easily into the biography of a few stout and earnest persons': Eliot telescopes these views

**sal volatile . . . brandy:** these restoratives may also be a concluding bathetic link between the sordid modern episode and Ariadne, who in one version of her story is found (abandoned in Naxos) by Dionysus, the god associated with wine, who revives and marries her

---

## A Cooking Egg

---

SUMMARY: Yet another meditation on time's decay, with the narrator, following hints that he is a fairly 'bad' fellow, revisiting a childhood acquaintance (evidently now a prim spinster) and feeling final regret and sorrow after the humorous list of his needs to be fulfilled by others in Heaven.

COMMENTARY: This elusive little poem has been given much attention by those anxious to identify the 'Cooking Egg' and the owner of the child- and bird-like name (nickname?) Pipit. After noting the nature of such an egg, together with the real 'bad egg' of the epigraph, and seeing what details about Pipit are hinted at in the poem (how proper she is, her 'distance' from the 'I', her spinsterly-seeming knitting, her sentimental Victorian possessions, her limited experience, the past link shown by the shared treat), the reader is best advised to follow the changes of tone from section to section: the rather sour amusement at the mixture of dignity and pathos in Pipit's situation; the comic whimsicality of the heavenly fancies, mockingly juxtaposing past and present; the serious final vision, regretting past losses and sorrowing over the tragic present. Once again it is the nature of the monologue itself, the nature of the mind here poetically dramatised, that is the real interest of the poem.

NOTES AND GLOSSARY:

| | |
|---|---|
| **title:** | an egg not fresh enough to be eaten on its own, if not yet entirely bad |
| **epigraph:** | the opening lines of the *Testament* of François Villon (1431–63 or later), looking back at his past sins: 'In the thirtieth year of my age/When I had drunk up all my shame' |
| **sate:** | an old-fashioned form of 'sat' for old-fashioned Pipit |
| **Views . . . Colleges:** | picture book |
| **Daguerreotypes:** | early photographic portraits of the last century; silhouettes are found even earlier |
| **Invitation to the Dance:** | suggests a sentimentally philistine taste in the arts, whether it is a picture or a piece of music |
| **Sir Philip Sidney:** | (1554–86), the heroic Elizabethan, an epitome of honour |
| **Coriolanus:** | this general became the proud hero of Shakespeare's last Roman play |
| **Sir Alfred Mond:** | (1868–1930), Jewish capitalist, a founder of Imperial Chemical Industries |
| **lapt:** | (*archaic*) wrapped |
| **Exchequer Bond:** | a British bond issued by the government at 5 per cent interest |
| **Lucretia Borgia:** | (1480–1519), a member of a powerful and notorious Italian family; several times married, she would certainly provide both 'Society' and entertainment |
| **Madame Blavatsky:** | (1831–91), a Russian spiritualist, a founder of the Theosophical Society |
| **Sacred Trances:** | an occult secret of Theosophy |
| **Piccarda de Donati:** | Dante (*Paradiso* III) is taught by this nun, forced to break her vows, at the lowest level of Heaven |
| **But where . . . Where . . .?:** | Eliot imitates the classical Latin rhetorical trick (*Ubi sunt . . .?*) of asking regretfully about past memories, a technique used in Villon's *Testament* (see epigraph) |
| **penny world:** | a trade expression for a cheap range of cakes and sweets |
| **behind the screen:** | where children ate in Victorian dining-rooms |
| **Kentish Town and Golders Green:** | North London suburbs |
| **eagles . . . Alps:** | evidently a reference to a failed Roman military expedition (the legions carried an eagle emblem) |
| **ABC's:** | London cafés owned by the Aerated Bread Company |

## The Hippopotamus

SUMMARY: A satirical contrast between the 'weak' hippo who goes to Heaven and the stagnant, self-righteous Church left below on earth.

COMMENTARY: This earliest of Eliot's quatrain poems shares the title of a poem by Gautier, and is the only one to use Gautier's full a-b-a-b rhyme-scheme; but where Gautier in *'L'Hippopotame'* likens himself to the hippo in fearless freedom, Eliot's animal is made, in a comical paradox, 'weak and frail' as any mortal flesh—yet (as with all sinners) standing for a better chance of salvation than the sleepy, rich, self-satisfied Church.

NOTES AND GLOSSARY:

**epigraph:** St Paul, writing here in his Epistle to the Colossians (4:16), urges that his words encouraging the faith of these early Christians should be sent on to the Laodiceans, who are described elsewhere in the —Bible (Revelation 3:16-17) as 'lukewarm' believers who say 'I am rich . . . and have need of nothing'— rather like Eliot's complacent Church

**rock:** Christ's pun on the name of St Peter and petra (*Greek* = rock): 'thou art Peter, and upon this rock I will build my church' (Matthew 16:18)

**God works . . . way:** adapted from a hymn by William Cowper (1731–1800), 'God moves in a mysterious way / His wonders to perform'

**quiring:** in a choir (*archaic*, quire)

**Blood of the Lamb:** the blood of Christ, the Lamb of God, sacrificed for the sins of the chosen who have 'washed their robes, and made them white in the blood of the Lamb' (Revelation 7:14)

**miasmal mist:** poisonous gas from rotting matter, which suggests a decaying Church smothered in the fog of error; Elizabeth Barrett Browning (1806–61) uses 'miasmal fog' in her poem *Aurora Leigh* (vii.717)

## Whispers of Immortality

SUMMARY: A Jacobean attitude linking death and sex is set against a modern separation: sex is restricted to a temptress, with her well-fleshed body, our metaphysical ('beyond the physical') ideas restricted to death, with its fleshless skeletons.

COMMENTARY: The change of style at mid-point, from morbid Jacobean gravity to colloquial lightness, emphasises the contrast between the two halves, though the 'dry ribs' that keep modern metaphysics going are effectively placed at the end to tie up with the 'breastless' skeletons at the beginning as well as Grishkin's welcoming bosom. Eliot is here poetically elaborating—in the loss of the seventeenth-century simultaneous apprehension of death-in-life, mind-and-body—one of his related critical beliefs, the 'dissociation of sensibility' (from his essay 'The Metaphysical Poets'): that whereas Donne and his fellows combine thought and feeling and 'feel their thought as immediately as the odour of a rose', later writers have lost this connective power.

NOTES AND GLOSSARY:

| | |
|---|---|
| **title:** | a fainter version of Wordsworth's 'Intimations of Immortality' |
| **Webster:** | (1580?–1625?), a dramatist noted for sensational imagery, much concerned with sex and death, in violent plots |
| **breastless . . . lipless:** | as of a skeleton |
| **Daffodil . . . eyes!:** | in Webster's tragedy *The White Devil* (V.4) there is 'A dead man's skull beneath the roots of flowers' |
| **pneumatic bliss:** | a joke derived from two aspects of a Greek word meaning 'of the spirit' or 'of wind', and so with associations both sacred (spiritual) and profane (as in a pneumatic drill) |
| **Abstract Entities:** | the joke here is that sexy Grishkin draws round her even the philosophers who deal in such abstract ideas of reality |
| **circumambulate:** | walk round as if shy of engaging |

## Mr Eliot's Sunday Morning Service

SUMMARY: This satire on the Church has three main points: it uses paradoxically neutral agents of reproduction to show how the Word of God (Christ) multiplies in the many words of the biblical commentators; it contrasts with these the painter's one simple and lasting image of the Trinity; and it attacks a Church that can make a living out of people from whom it seems remote.

COMMENTARY: The learnedness of this ecclesiastical extravaganza must, despite the humour, frighten off more readers than it ever entertains, but is appropriate to the subject Notice Eliot's characteristic use of sexual images to present mental and spiritual states, and the further links provided throughout the poem by, for instance, pictures (the window-panes may show a troop of divines in stained glass as well as the bees; there is the central religious painting; and there is the suggestion of another painting in the angel-supported gateway to Purgatory in the sixth stanza) and word play (the last word looks back to the first monstrosity). The final introduction of Sweeney gives a shock when we are expecting 'Mr Eliot': shifting in his bath he grotesquely parodies both baptism and the shifts of the scholars, yet without any application to such ordinary mortals the whole theological debate is meaningless, as meaningless as the obscure words would be to such people (if not Mr Eliot). By an appropriate contrast, Sweeney and the painting in the third and fourth stanzas are much more easily understood.

NOTES AND GLOSSARY:

**epigraph:** as in 'Portrait of a Lady', from Marlowe's *The Jew of Malta* (V.1); here the Jew's servant sees two friars, 'caterpillars' who feed off society

**Polyphiloprogenitive:** wanting many offspring; Eliot added a 'poly' (=many) to a word used in the 1865 English translation of *A New Life of Jesus* (II, 41) by David Friedrich Strauss (1808–74), relating God, in the mystery of the begetting of Jesus, to the 'philoprogenitive Gods of the heathen'

**sapient sutlers:** the (would-be) wise sellers of provisions to an army, in this case the learned scholars who provide the Lord's soldiers with arguments about the Bible

**In the beginning was the Word:** Christ as the Word; see the Bible, the opening of St John's Gospel, which continues, '. . . and the Word was God'

**Superfetation . . .:** multiple fertilisation (and hence multiple births) of 'the One' (*Greek*)—nicely illustrated by the preceding identical repetition

**mensual turn:** (due) month

**enervate Origen:** this seminal Christian theologian (*c*.185–*c*.254) was believed to have castrated himself, the better to father a reputed 6,000 religious books; his teachings, particularly on the problematical relationship of Christ, God the Son, to God the Father, in turn produced numerous controversies

**Umbrian school:** Italian school of painting, at its peak in the fifteenth century under the leadership of Perugino (*c*.1450–1523)

**gesso ground:** plaster surface prepared for a wall painting

**Baptised God:** Christ was baptised by John the Baptist in the River Jordan—a popular subject in Western art, with the other two Persons of the Trinity usually looking down from above

| | |
|---|---|
| **Paraclete:** | the Comforter, or God the Holy Ghost (represented in painting as a dove) |
| **sable presbyters:** | black-clothed elders of the Church (Origen was an ordained presbyter) |
| **piaculative pence:** | the payment for their probably sexual sins, by which the repentant, pimply young churchgoers hope to earn forgiveness |
| **invisible and dim:** | a phrase from 'The Night', by the devout poet Henry Vaughan (1622–95) |
| **bees:** | linked with the sutlers as fertilising agents for flowers, taking pollen from stamen to pistil |
| **epicene:** | neuter, with characteristics of both sexes or no sexual characteristic, as are—despite their fertilising function—Origen and the worker bees |

---

## Sweeney Among the Nightingales

---

SUMMARY: Ape-like Sweeney is here relaxing in some low den, but the two females are thought to be plotting against him and tension mounts as the other men draw away from him—then the poem sweeps on to recall a classical murder.

COMMENTARY: This dramatic poem advances in a remarkable series of shifts. The low-key opening immediately gives way to that 'sense of foreboding' that Eliot once said was all he consciously set out to create in the poem. For a while the spectacle of the fallen woman in the cape and the staring man in brown lift the tension, but as the thirty-two lines of the long final sentence gather momentum, the details become ominous and threatening: the brown man's withdrawal; the accomplice's murderousness; the departure (and reappearance at the window, with his sinister gold-toothed smile) of the man who has rejected an advance; the distant host talking to a dark figure. Before anything happens to Sweeney, the eternal nightingales prelude the sombre grandeur of that ancient murder. It seems very much in line with Eliot's usual contrast of sordid present and heroic past, but this time there is a strangely moving link established between Sweeney and the equally human and 'maculate' Agamemnon.

As for the other links that weld the poem together, you may notice such things as the characteristic sexual possibilities of certain phrases such as 'spreads his knees', 'hornèd gate', 'vertebrate . . . withdraws', or the chosen fruits, and the eerie imagery (the moon, the sea, the wood, and so on) that is also so often animal: not only the prominent nightingale motifs, but the ape, zebra and giraffe attributes of Sweeney, the evil omens of Raven and Dog (always menacing in Eliot), the man seen as merely 'vertebrate', Rachel's 'paws'. In all, a striking conclusion to the 1920 volume, with power rising above puzzle.

NOTES AND GLOSSARY:

**title:** this recalls Elizabeth Barrett Browning's 'Bianca Among the Nightingales', a poem in which nightingales 'sing through death', as they do at the end of Eliot's poem; 'nightingales' is also a slang term for prostitutes, among whom Sweeney is placed in the poem

**epigraph:** 'Alas, I am struck deep with a mortal blow': from the *Agamemnon* (line 1343) of the Greek tragedian Aeschylus (525–456BC), the cry of King Agamemnon as he is murdered by his adulterous wife, plotting with her lover

**maculate:** spotted (as a giraffe, and implying the sinfully spotted who are not 'immaculate')

**circles . . . moon:** circles round the moon foretell storms

**River Plate:** or Plata, in South America; its name implies the riches expected in its hinterland

**Raven:** a constellation; this bird proverbially forebodes death

**hornèd gate:** true dreams, in classical mythology, pass from the underworld through a gate of horn to get to man, false ones through a gate of ivory

**Orion . . . Dog:** the constellation of Orion (the Hunter) includes the Dog Star (Sirius)

**man in mocha brown:** may be a returned First World War soldier in khaki, as Agamemnon was a returned hero from the Trojan War

**Rachel née Rabinovitch:** another of Eliot's nasty Jews

**nightingales . . . bloody wood:** Eliot said he was thinking of the grove of the Furies at Colonus: 'I called it "bloody" because of the blood of Agamemnon in Argos'; in *Oedipus at Colonus* by Sophocles (459–406BC) this grove is filled with nightingales that sing as Oedipus goes to his death, and in the *Agamemnon* Aeschylus uses the image of the betrayed nightingale in a prophecy of death

**the Sacred Heart:** of Christ, stressing his suffering for humanity

**liquid siftings:** of excrement

# *The Hollow Men* (1925)

This work was built up from a number of separate poems; the first four sections appeared separately and in different combinations until the addition of the last section (in *Poems 1909-1925*) gave us the poem as we now have it. Its manner of composition is found also in the next poem, *Ash-Wednesday*, and may account for some of the apparent discrepancies between the sections of both poems that cause local difficulties of interpretation, but the shared metrical and emotional characteristics of the sequences weld each into a coherent poetic unity—and it is grasping that overall effect, rather than puzzling over isolated uncertainties, at which the newcomer to such poems should aim.

Though Eliot said he got the title by combining 'The Hollow Land', a romance by William Morris (1834-96), with 'The Broken Men', a poem by Rudyard Kipling (1865-1936), it may be more helpful to remember that Shakespeare gives the phrase 'hollow men' to Brutus (*Julius Caesar* IV.2), as he is pondering the deceitful weakness of his fellow assassin, Cassius. This would link up with the treachery associated with the second epigraph (see below) and the recollection of another speech by Brutus in Part V of the poem. Further associations with 'hollow' men are provided by the first epigraph (see below). The poem has two epigraphs, on consecutive pages in *Selected Poems*.

'Mistah Kurtz—he dead' is the uneducated announcement of an insolent servant in *Heart of Darkness* (1899), a great story by Joseph Conrad (1857-1924) that had a deep effect on Eliot, who thought it an outstanding literary treatment of evil. Set mainly in the darkness of the African jungle, the story explores the darkness at the heart of the so-called civilised men who were sent out there by the European nations during the nineteenth-century 'Scramble for Africa'. Kurtz is such a man, a 'universal genius' who is all the more surely taken over by the darkness, and just before his death is announced he has a vision of this: 'The horror! The horror!' he cries, in words that Eliot planned to use as an epigraph to *The Waste Land*, from discarded bits of which parts of this poem were developed. Even Kurtz, in a story full of hollow men, is described as 'hollow at the core', a 'hollow sham'.

The second epigraph is a version of a chant still used by children begging money for fireworks as they cart about their 'guy', an effigy of Guy Fawkes wearing old clothes and stuffed with straw or paper. This is set alight (as are the fireworks) on the night of Guy Fawkes Day (5 November), the anniversary of the 'Gunpowder Plot' of Roman Catholics to blow up King James and his ministers at the Houses of Parliament on 5 November 1605: on the night before, Guy Fawkes was arrested in the cellar of the House of Lords, guarding nearly two tons of gunpowder.

## Part I

SUMMARY: The hopeless state of these empty, passive lives.

COMMENTARY: Notice how the short lines and the repetitions, varied by rhymes and partial rhymes (men ... men ... when; together ... together ... cellar; Alas ... less ... grass ... glass), emphasise the feebleness and limitedness and pointlessness being presented. The verse structure, different from that of any of the earlier poems, helps to set the tone of the poem as much as the images that will be developed.

NOTES AND GLOSSARY:

**hollow men:** see notes above on the title

**stuffed men ... straw:** image from the stuffed guy: see note above on the second epigraph

**dry cellar:** part of the hopeless and sordid imagery, primarily, but also setting up possible associations with the cellar where Guy Fawkes kept his powder dry

**shape without form ... motion:** four images of things that have lost their essential meaning, like everything about these people: a shape without form is shapeless, and so on

**death's other Kingdom:** the first of several kingdoms in the poem, this capitalised Kingdom suggests the one to which the souls of the blessed pass after death. It is 'other' than the kingdom here on earth of the living dead, the hollow men, who will in turn join the hopeless band of not very good, not very bad souls that in Dante (*Hell* III) are not accepted for Heaven, nor for purging in Purgatory, nor even for Hell (which wants the decisively bad—the 'lost/Violent souls') because they have been tepid and indecisive in their lives. While the damned cross the River Acheron to Hell, these tepid souls are condemned to stay eternally by the river, a ghastly Limbo. (Eliot thought it was actually better for humans 'to do evil than to do nothing: at least, we exist')

**Violent souls:** perhaps such as Guy Fawkes or Kurtz or Caesar's assassins, decisively 'lost' or damned, unlike the tepidly undecided 'we'

## Part II

SUMMARY: The timidity of one, afraid of righteous reproach after death, who wishes to be left with his fragmentary, distant vision—a scarecrow flapping in the wind.

COMMENTARY: In this section a personalised 'I' takes up a number of images used by the 'we' in the first section and develops them. The 'direct eyes' here cannot be faced even in dreams (sleep imitates death), and do not appear in the waking nightmare of living death, where one has only partial glimpses of another life; nor does the 'I' wish to come nearer those reproachful eyes, as he must do in death. The 'other Kingdom' of Part I is contrasted with this 'dream kingdom' of living death and the intermediate 'twilight kingdom' where one's appointed destination (Heaven, Purgatory, Hell, Limbo) is decided. Other developments include the 'hollow', 'stuffed' dummy image (in the cellar with rats) that is developed into a scarecrow image (in a field with a dead rat).

NOTES AND GLOSSARY:

**Eyes:** significant in both Dante and *Heart of Darkness*

**death's dream kingdom** (twice): this kingdom seems to be closest to the 'real' world of the hollow men

**There** (twice): ambiguous, but seems to refer to the partial vision that sees, not the eyes of the blessed (as in Beatrice's eyes, which Dante at first shame-facedly avoids in *Purgatory*, especially cantos XXX and XXXI), but fragments of that life on the other side of death

**twilight kingdom:** evidently some transitional state (such states are prominent in Eliot: intermediate colours such as violet, intermediate times of day such as twilight and dawn, and so forth) between this life and the next, particularly, perhaps, the time of dying itself

**Rat's coat, crowskin:** refers to the farmer's custom of hanging up corpses of pests to frighten off others

**crossed staves:** of a scarecrow, moved about by the wind

## Part III

SUMMARY: The desert waste, where useless idols receive the attention of the loveless.

COMMENTARY: Notice the development of the images of decay and meaninglessness from the 'broken glass' (which has lost its usefulness) in Part I, through the 'broken column' glimpsed in Part II, to the 'broken stone' here of a useless stone idol: the man who prays to such an image is already doomed to death. For the first time, a hint of suppressed sexual love is clearly given ('Waking alone . . . kiss'), throwing further light on the dried-up condition of the hollow men.

NOTES AND GLOSSARY:
**dead land . . . cactus land:** wasteland images of this living death on earth

**stone images . . . broken stone:** as in 'your images shall be broken . . .
your idols may be broken', in the Bible, Ezekiel
6:4, 6

**death's other kingdom:** it is hard to know whether the lower-case 'k' is
intended to distinguish this other kingdom of death
from that in Part I; perhaps this kingdom is where
all the damned dead go

**Lips that would kiss/Form prayers . . .:** evidently as a second-best
activity, as in a line by James Thomson (1834-82)
from his poem 'Art', 'Lips only sing when they cannot kiss'; there is also Juliet's 'lips that they [the
holy] must use in prayer [not kissing]' (*Romeo and
Juliet*, I.5)

---

## Part IV

---

SUMMARY: The end of these lost lives, for whom there is no blessed
vision.

COMMENTARY: The culmination of the eyes and star and death and
hollow men imagery is found here, with the clearest indications of both
the damned waiting by the river of Hell and the blessed with their star
and rose.

NOTES AND GLOSSARY:

**broken jaw:** image of desolation and lack of ability to communicate; and a possible contrast with the unbroken
'jawbone of an ass' with which Samson slew a
thousand Philistines. See the Bible, Judges 15:15

**our lost kingdoms:** not of death this time, but of men, and their illusions

**tumid river:** corresponds with Dante's presentation (*Hell* III) of
the River Acheron that flows round Hell: on the
bank ('beach'), their last meeting place, the souls
of the dead wait to be ferried across

**the perpetual star:** a contrast with the 'fading' and 'dying' stars earlier
in the poem, this description recalls both the 'living
star' of Dante's vision of the Virgin Mary (*Heaven*
XXIII, 92) and the 'single star' (XXXI, 28) of the
Light of God

**Multifoliate rose:** recalls Dante's vision of the highest Heaven as a
rose, with the Virgin and other saints forming the
many petals (*foglia* is 'petal' in Italian) in *Heaven*
XXX and the following Cantos, but Mary herself
is described as a rose in Canto XXIII, 73—just
before she is called a 'living star' (see previous note)

**death's twilight kingdom:** a transitional region (see note on 'twilight kingdom' in Part II above) where (only) the hollow men have still the (vain) hope of seeing the beatific vision

**only:** perhaps deliberately ambiguous, this could mean the vision is only the hope (not the actual fate) of the empty men or/and only such men would have such a hope; it would be hard to make it mean the blessed vision is their 'only hope', especially as all they can expect (hope for) is a hopeless existence as in Dante's Limbo

## Part V

SUMMARY: The final vision of the meaningless round of unfulfilled lives, broken speaking of the highest Kingdom, and the pathetic end of this world.

COMMENTARY: In this final section the most notable feature is one of tone change, both in the change from the previous sections and the changes within the conclusion itself. The critic F.R. Leavis (1895–1978) finely observed the 'nightmare poise over the grotesque'* here, which applies to the whole balancing act that can move from the bizarre opening chant to the sombre truth of the intervening Shadow, and on through the meditative fragments to the final chant's 'whimper'. The last Kingdom is the highest, the Kingdom of God: the poet, barely able to approach even the thought of it, stammers out broken phrases. The broken lives presented throughout the poem fade away in a conclusion combining a feeble trailing off with a memorable inevitability.

It is Eliot's bleakest poetic vision, a vision of dry lives lacking the clear element of hope (the promise of rain) which even 'Gerontion' and *The Waste Land* have. From now on, however, the way can only be upwards.

NOTES AND GLOSSARY:

**Here we go round ... morning:** a parody of a children's chant, imitating 'Here we go round the mulberry bush' and 'Here we go gathering nuts in May', both originating in fertility dances

**prickly pear:** this cactus, flourishing in desert soil, gives a pointed twist to the expected fertility symbol

**five o'clock ...:** the traditional hour of Christ's resurrection; dawn dances are common in Mayday and other rituals of the cycles of renewal after death

*In *New Bearings in English Poetry*, Penguin Books, Harmondsworth, 1963, p.96.

**Between the idea . . . the Shadow:** the Shadow is whatever in men's lives, after something is proposed, prevents its realisation, coming between what might be and what actually is: between a desire and its fulfilment, and so on

**motion . . . act:** recalls the words of Brutus (in Shakespeare's *Julius Caesar* II.1): 'Between the acting of a dreadful thing/And the first motion, all the interim is/Like a phantasma, or a hideous dream'

**Falls the Shadow:** Eliot agreed that he derived this phrase from the best-known poem by Ernest Dowson (1867–1900), 'Non sum qualis eram bonae sub regno Cynarae' (Horace: 'I am not as I was beneath the reign of good Cynara'), in which we find 'There fell thy shadow' and 'Then falls thy shadow'. Other relevant associations of shadow may be found in many places elsewhere, from the tormenting shadows of *Heart of Darkness* back to 'the valley of the shadow of death' in Psalm 23

*For Thine is the Kingdom:* from the Lord's Prayer ('Our Father'); the ultimate capitalised Kingdom of God

*Life is very long:* this phrase appears in Conrad's novel *The Outcast of the Islands* (1896), where a broken man is to be punished by being kept alive rather than killed; it reads in the poem as an exhausted reversal of the usual idea—that life is short but art is long. For 'conception' and 'creation', 'emotion' and 'response' apply as much to art as to life; indeed, at one level the poem is a commentary on artistic as well as spiritual and sexual sterility

**essence . . . descent:** according to the Greek philosopher Plato (*c*.428–*c*.348BC), the essence or ideal, spiritual form descends to a lower material reality to take physical form

**This is the way . . . :** the parodied children's song returns, as in 'This is the way we (clap our hands)'

**Not with a bang:** as hoped for by Guy Fawkes, or those with visions of a grand violence at earth's end, or those who idiomatically wish to go out (from life, a job, etcetera) 'with a bang', that is, impressively; the phrase also recalls the account by George Santayana (1863–1952), who taught Eliot at Harvard, of the *Divine Comedy*'s ending 'not with a bang, not with some casual incident, but in sustained reflection'

| | |
|---|---|
| **whimper:** | this feeble sound contrasts appropriately with a bang. In Rudyard Kipling's poem 'Danny Deever', the soul of a soldier executed for cowardice 'whimpers' overhead as it passes; Eliot thought Kipling's choice of 'whimpers' was 'exactly right' |

## Ash-Wednesday (1930)

This and the remaining poems in *Selected Poems* were all published after Eliot's reception into the Church of England as a convert (Latin *convertere*, to turn about). The title refers to the first day of Lent, the forty days of fasting (as Christ fasted in the wilderness) and turning from sin towards godliness that precede the Easter celebration of Christ's resurrection. The poem is full of references to the liturgy of this day, named from the traditional ash cross marked by the priest on the foreheads of the congregation. For instance, the poem takes up the reading for the Epistle that begins at Joel 2:12: 'Turn ye even to me, saith the Lord'.

### Part I

SUMMARY: The convert renounces everything in his past in order to learn the passive way to God.

COMMENTARY: The simple words and repetitions immediately effect an impression of the 'small and dry' voice of a man struggling to make clear what is complex, as in the simple language used to utter deep thoughts in Dante and the Bible and Roman Catholic and Anglican liturgy, the three underlying sources of the entire poem.

NOTES AND GLOSSARY:

| | |
|---|---|
| **Because I do not hope to turn again:** | a translation of 'Perch 'io non spero di tornar giammai', the opening line of a poem by the Italian Guido Cavalcanti (1255–1300) lamenting his exile and expecting never to see his lady again. When Part I was first published, as a separate poem, it was entitled 'Perch 'io Non Spero' |
| **Desiring . . . scope:** | a version ('gift' instead of 'art') of a line from Shakespeare's Sonnet 29, where the poet's discontent with his lot turns to joy when he thinks of his beloved. A renunciation of poetry seems to be implied in this section—or at least of the former type of poetry |
| **agèd eagle:** | reputed to be able to renew its youth and vigour (as in Psalm 103) |

| | |
|---|---|
| **infirm glory:** | a phrase used in *Night and Day* (1919), a novel by Virginia Woolf (1882–1941), to refer to the once-famous, now old |
| **time . . . place:** | implied contrasts with eternity and infinity |
| **blessèd face:** | in rejecting even this (which recalls especially the face of Dante's Beatrice), the convert rejects both an earlier love and a beatific vision as a way of turning to God |
| **the voice:** | including his own former poetic voice? |
| **vans:** | not only an archaic word for 'wings', this also means the 'fans' which are used in winnowing chaff from grain |
| **to care:** | about godly things |
| **not to care:** | about worldly things that need to be renounced |
| **to sit still:** | the passive way for the soul to prepare for God, as described by the Spanish mystic, St John of the Cross (1542–91); in his *Pensées*, the French philosopher and physicist Blaise Pascal (1623–62) thinks 'all the troubles of man come from his not knowing how to sit still' |
| **Pray for us . . . death:** | conclusion of a prayer to the Virgin Mary, asking her to plead with God for sinners |

---

## Part II

---

SUMMARY: Addressing the Lady, the convert, dead to his former life, rejoices in his dry bones.

COMMENTARY: When first published separately, Part II was entitled 'Salutation'. This underlines the links with both Beatrice (who salutes Dante in *The New Life*, III, dressed in pure white) and the Virgin (saluted by the Angel Gabriel as well as the devout): as in Dante, a parallel between these two Ladies is established in the poem, and they are basic to its total imagery. But the imagery is not necessarily limited by such specific references: the Rose also recalls the whole courtly love tradition implied by the medieval *Romance of the Rose*, the Garden also recalls the Garden of Eden, and so forth.

NOTES AND GLOSSARY:

| | |
|---|---|
| **Lady:** | recalls Beatrice, agent of Dante's salvation, and devoted attendant on the Virgin Mary in Paradise |
| **white:** | colour of purity used for three descriptions in this section: leopards, Lady, bones |
| **leopards:** | here seeming to destroy on God's orders, as in the Bible (for example, Jeremiah 5:6) |

**juniper-tree:** this symbol of cleansing and rebirth appears in 'The Juniper-Tree', a fairy tale retold by the German Brothers Grimm, Jacob (1785–1863) and Wilhelm (1786–1859), in which a murdered child's bones, put beneath a juniper, are miraculously restored to life; another miracle appears in the biblical story of Elijah, who prayed for death under a juniper in the wilderness and was sent food by God instead (1 Kings 19:1–8)

**my legs . . . skull:** organs representing activity, emotion, sensuality and thought

**shall these bones . . .:** in the vision of Ezekiel in the valley of dry bones, God asks 'can these bones live?' before restoring them to life. See the Bible, Ezekiel 37:3

**dissembled:** a pun on disguised and dis-assembled; in pieces

**fruit of the gourd:** of which the inside is taken out so that the rind can be dried and made useful

**Prophesy to the wind:** the words of God in Ezekiel 37:9, to put breath back into the bodies made from the restored bones

**bones sang:** appears twice, as does 'chirping', to stress the happiness, as in Psalm 51 (often sung on Ash-Wednesday in addition to the 'Proper' Psalms): 'Make me to hear joy and gladness; that the bones which thou hast broken may rejoice'

**burden:** (*a*) plague; (*b*) tune: a punning allusion to 'the grasshopper shall be a burden'; see the Bible, Ecclesiastes 12:5

**Lady of silences . . . all love ends:** an imitation of the Litany of the Blessed Virgin Mary, where she is addressed as 'Rose', 'Mother', and so on; Eliot's idea of the paradoxical combination of opposites ('Calm and distressed' etcetera) is presumably developed from her essential paradox as Virgin and Mother

**in the cool of the day:** description of God's walk in the Garden of Eden. See the Bible, Genesis 3:8

**This is the land . . . lot:** God's words in Ezekiel 48:29

## Part III

SUMMARY: The turnings of the convert's spiritual progress are here imaged in the climbing of a staircase.

COMMENTARY: At its first, separate publication, Part III was entitled 'Som de L'Escalina' ('The top of the staircase'). These words are from a speech addressed to Dante, as he ascends the third section of the stairway through *Purgatory* (XXVI, 146), by the Provençal poet Arnaut Daniel (*fl. c.*1200) sent there for lustfulness. This section develops both the staircase image and the idea that sensual distractions hinder spiritual progress. These memories, lovingly recalled, contrast vividly with the 'old man' and 'agèd shark' of the spiritual struggle.

NOTES AND GLOSSARY:

**same shape:**    as himself, in an earlier struggle

**devil ... despair:**    Eliot thought the 'demon of doubt' is 'inseparable from the spirit of belief'

**fig's fruit:**    begins a series of distracting recollections of the sensuous world

**figure ... flute:**    a medievalised pagan figure, perhaps to be associated with Pan, the amorous and pipe-playing god of pastoral life in Greek mythology

**Lilac:**    as the context shows, the flower is associated with a memory of past love

**Lord, I am not worthy ... only:** the words of humility spoken in the Mass, from Matthew 8:8: 'Lord, I am not worthy that thou shouldst come under my roof: but speak the word only and my servant shall be healed' (in liturgical use, 'soul' can be substituted for 'servant')

---

## Part IV

---

SUMMARY: In the peace of the garden, a nun-like figure wordlessly signals a message of redemption.

COMMENTARY: The chief problem of interpretation has always been the relationship of the veiled sister and the Lady of Part II: all we can say, looking ahead to the rest of the poem, is that both are associated with Mary and Beatrice; more specific identification is probably restricting, though tempting. For it may be that the very obscurity and impersonality of this section reveals a too personal association that Eliot is covering up, as he did when removing the original dedication of the poem, 'To My Wife'. Some readers, for instance, see a reference to Vivienne's hospitalisation, the 'sister' being a nursing sister, a role often taken by nuns. But there are only hints, and perhaps the reader should concentrate on the public 'meaning' of the poem throughout.

NOTES AND GLOSSARY:

**violet:**    (*a*) the colour is associated with both transition and repentance; (*b*) the flower is associated with both resurrection and purity

**Mary's colour:** blue; but sometimes also white

**trivial:** may include a pun on the origin of this word: where *three roads* meet, the basic experiences of learning and life (see the three dreams in Part VI)

**ignorance ... knowledge:** not knowing such suffering in herself, perhaps, yet knowing of the suffering of others

**larkspur:** blue flower (delphinium)

**Sovegna vos:** 'Be mindful', the plea of Arnaut Daniel (*Purgatory* XXVI, 147) that the punishment for lust should be kept in mind by Dante (See Part III, Commentary, above)

**Redeem/The time:** by, as St Paul advised in his Epistles, using one's time wisely

**the higher dream:** in his 'Dante' essay, Eliot associates the Divine Pageant in *Purgatory* XXIX, in which Beatrice's chariot is drawn by a griffon, with 'the world of what I call the *high dream*, and the modern world seems capable only of the *low dream*'. The hearse in the next line seems to mourn the passing of the higher dream

**veiled:** as are nuns, followers of Mary, and Beatrice; also mourners

**yews:** trees associated with churchyards, and hence death

**garden god ... flute:** suggests Pan once more (see Part III, note)

**And after this our exile:** from the *Salve Regina* ('Hail, Queen'), a prayer to the Virgin continuing 'show unto us the blessed fruit of thy womb, Jesus'

---

## Part V

---

SUMMARY: A lamentation for those who do not hear and surrender to the Word of God.

COMMENTARY: The word-play in Part V is often criticised as excessive, not so much in the opening Andrewes-style turning round and round of particular phrases to be examined as in the elaborate internal rhymes ('found ... Resound', 'mainland ... rainland', etcetera) of the central passages.

NOTES AND GLOSSARY:

**The Word without a word:** part of a development based on the opening of St John's Gospel and the Christmas 1618 sermon of Lancelot Andrewes: see notes on the similar usage in 'Gerontion'

**And the light ...:** as in the Bible, John 1:5

**world . . . whirled:** a pun found in *Orchestra*, a poem by John Davies (1565–1618): 'Behold the world, how it is whirled round!'

**unstilled:** because ever-turning, as well as ever-disobedient to the Word

**O my people . . . thee:** from the Bible, Micah 6:3, used in Christ's Reproaches from the Cross in the Good Friday liturgy

**affirm:** the faith

**deny:** the old life

**desert in the garden:** the death of the old life of sensuous delights but spiritual emptiness

**garden in the desert:** the spiritual rebirth brought about by desolation and suffering

## Part VI

SUMMARY: The convert acknowledges the pull of his past life, but prays for help to find peace with God.

COMMENTARY: The opening 'Although' takes us back to the 'Because' of Part I and adds its qualification: although he hopes his conversion is final, the convert clearly recognises the pull of old desires, movingly presented in the memories of the sea and the love he has lost. As the time of conversion (the dying of the old man and the birth of the new) is difficult, the help of the blessed teachers is needed. Here the poet brings together all the previous female presences in the poem to aid his final prayer.

Much may have been unclear or laboured, much may have seemed to depend on biblical, liturgical and Dante-esque catch phrases that can do the poet's work for him, much may have been hard to swallow for those who do not share Eliot's renunciatory attitude—but as an enacted vision of the convert, with its cumulative power of imagery and incantation, *Ash-Wednesday* can also be deeply moving.

NOTES AND GLOSSARY:

**dreamcrossed twilight . . . dying:** as in the 'twilight kingdom' in 'The Hollow Men'

**Bless me father** [for I have sinned]: opening words of the penitent to the priest at Confession

**lost lilac:** once again a memory of lost love

**golden-rod:** long-stemmed plant with yellow flowers

**ivory gates:** through which false dreams pass from the underworld to earth; such delusions are created by the eye that is blind to the true Word

| | |
|---|---|
| **three dreams:** | perhaps three such hopes of fulfilment as the artistic, the sexual and the spiritual; perhaps three such states of desire as consciousness, memory and dream, etcetera |
| **the other yew:** | this tree is a symbol of immortality as well as death |
| **sit still:** | see note on this phrase in Part I |

**Our peace in his will:** the words of the nun Piccarda (see 'A Cooking Egg') in *Paradiso* III, 85

**Suffer me . . . separated** [from Thee]: from the ancient hymn *Anima Christi* ('Soul of Christ')

**And let my cry . . . Thee:** liturgical response to the priest's words, 'Hear my prayer, O Lord' (from Psalm 102)

# *Ariel Poems*

The four poems in this section were published by Faber and Faber in successive years as a kind of Christmas card. The first three have clear Christmas associations, with the first two relating specifically to the birth of Christ, and the rather different Shakespearean fourth records another miraculous event.

## Journey of the Magi (1927)

SUMMARY: One of the Magi, recalling their hard journey, unexpectedly describes not the joyful but the saddening and hard-to-bear results.

COMMENTARY: As in 'Gerontion', this is the monologue of an old man reviewing the past; as in *Ash-Wednesday*, he and his companions have to struggle against the old life: not only when the tough journey made them long for summer, silken girls, sherbet (a refreshing drink); not only the difficult acceptance of the Word; but even the suffering caused by alienation from their own people, still holding to their heathen gods. The journey is not over yet.

The imagery of the middle section is particularly unusual, both for the prophetic suggestions of future events of the Crucifixion (a literary technique called *prolepsis*) and for the significance of the choice of the other images. Of such apparently random but emotion-charged images Eliot has written illuminatingly:

> six ruffians seen through an open window playing cards at night at a small French railway junction where there was a watermill: such memories may have symbolic value, but of what we cannot tell, for they come to represent the depths of feeling into which we cannot peer.*

*In *The Use of Poetry and the Use of Criticism*, Faber & Faber, London, 1964, p.148.

NOTES AND GLOSSARY:

**Magi:** the three wise men who came from the East with gifts for the newly-born Jesus. See the Bible, Matthew 2:1–12

**'A cold . . . of winter':** the quoted words are adapted from the 1622 Christmas Day sermon by Bishop Andrewes: 'A cold coming they had of it at this time of the year, just the worst time of the year to take a journey, and specially a long journey in. The ways deep, the weather sharp . . . "the very dead of winter"'

**three trees:** there were to be three crosses at the Crucifixion, for Christ and the two thieves

**white horse:** in the Bible, Revelation 19:11, Christ rides a white horse in glory

**dicing . . . silver:** the Roman soldiers diced for the clothes of the crucified Christ, who was betrayed for thirty pieces of silver

**set down/This:** a phrase used by Andrewes in the same sermon (and elsewhere); here the old Magus is addressing his implied listener(s), anxious that no aspect of his story should be missed

**Birth or Death:** because one must 'die' to the old life before being 'born' to the new life in Christ: see *Ash-Wednesday*

**these Kingdoms:** traditionally the Magi were also kings

**the old dispensation:** that is, pre-Christ

**another death:** into eternal life this time (as promised by Christ)?

---

## A Song for Simeon (1928)

---

SUMMARY: A development of the biblical Song of Simeon.

COMMENTARY: This is another monologue of a tired old man, waiting for death, but he is much more peaceful and accepting than Gerontion, and the movement of the verse is even more simple and gentle than that of the old Magus in the previous poem. Notice how this effect is assisted by repeating rhymes more than once: 'and', 'stand', 'hand', 'land' and so on. However, the simplicity does not preclude the possibility of sophisticated metrics, notably in the placing of the biblical extracts, and complex imagery, notably in the opening verse paragraph.

NOTES AND GLOSSARY:

**Simeon:** in the Bible story this 'just and devout' Jew, promised by the Holy Ghost that he shall not die before he has seen Christ, takes the baby in his arms in the temple and can die happy. His Song is sung at

Evening Prayer (*Nunc dimittis*): 'Lord, now lettest thou thy servant depart in peace, according to thy word: for mine eyes have seen thy salvation, which thou hast prepared before the face of all people; a light to lighten the Gentiles, and the glory of thy people Israel'; see the Bible, Luke 2:29-32. The poem repeats phrases from this canticle, and develops other ideas in Simeon's story

**Lord:** as in the Bible Song, Simeon's first word

**Roman:** Judaea was then under Roman rule

**hyacinths:** spring flowers of death and rebirth, but here artificially grown indoors in the winter: an image of Simeon's amazing 'spring' in the winter of his old age

**Grant . . . peace:** a liturgical echo of Simeon's prayer

**time of sorrow:** Simeon begins looking ahead to the persecution of the Christians: in the Bible, Luke 2:34-5, he prophesies the suffering to come

**cords and scourges:** as used when Christ was whipped by the Romans

**stations:** hints at the Stations of the Cross (events of the Crucifixion)

**mountain of desolation:** the hill of Calvary, but, as in all these images, capable of extension to the later sufferings of Christ's followers

**maternal sorrow:** Mary witnessed the Crucifixion

**birth season of decease:** a typical play on the idea of dying into life, especially appropriate to this very old man

**Infant . . . Word:** more verbal play derived from the *Verbum Infans* sermon (1618) of Andrewes: see notes to 'Gerontion'

**saints' stair:** see *Ash-Wednesday* III

**Not for me . . .:** he will not himself experience the suffering and the ecstatic vision of the Christian saints and martyrs

**(And a sword . . . also):** in Luke 2:35, Simeon warns Mary in just such a parenthesis: '(Yea, a sword shall pierce through thy own soul also)'; once more, of course, Eliot's usage is capable of extension, even to the reader

## Animula (1929)

SUMMARY: The progress of the soul from the explorations of childhood to the paralysis grown from experience.

COMMENTARY: Some readers find the rhythms, if not the rhymes, rather monotonous, and the poem generally lacking in poetic (as opposed to philosophic) energy and inventiveness. But the child's eye view of the world is sensitively recreated, and the different last section can come to seem, with familiarity, more suggestive than mystifying.

NOTES AND GLOSSARY:

**Animula:** a little soul, as in the first line of a poem addressed to his soul by the Emperor Hadrian (76–138): 'Animula vagula blandula' ('Little soul, wandering, pleasing')

**'Issues . . . soul':** this quotation derives from a passage in Dante's *Purgatory* discussing the nature of the soul and its need of control; Eliot gives the following translation in his 'Dante' essay of Canto XVI, lines 85 to 96: 'From the hands of Him who loves her before she is, there issues like a little child that plays, with weeping and laughter, the simple soul, that knows nothing except that, come from the hands of a glad creator, she turns willingly to everything that delights her. First she tastes the flavour of a trifling good; then is beguiled, and pursues it, if neither guide nor check withhold her. Therefore laws were needed as a curb; a ruler was needed, who should at least see afar the tower of the true City'

**fragrant brilliance:** combining the scent of the tree with its bright decorations

**running stags:** may include a reference to the legendary Actaeon, the hunter turned into a stag and killed by his own hounds (see also the second last line of the poem)

**imperatives:** moral considerations that impel us to action

**'is and seems':** as in *Appearance and Reality* (1893), by the philosopher F.H. Bradley (1846–1924), on whom Eliot completed a Harvard thesis in 1916: the difference between appearance ('seems') and reality ('is')

***Encyclopaedia Britannica:*** the largest and best-known encyclopaedia in English

**Issues . . . time . . .:** this variation of the first line begins the stage where experience (time) has distorted the soul

**Denying . . . blood:** rejecting the impulsive demands of feeling

**viaticum:** (*a*) communion given to the dying, from (*b*) what is provided for the soul's sustenance on its journey

**Guiterriez:** Eliot intended this to represent (especially by onomatopoeia?) the 'successful person of the machine age'

| | |
|---|---|
| **Boudin:** | similarly intended to represent (from the French slang sense, 'explosive', of a word used normally for a blood pudding, which has the shape of a sausage—'banger' in English slang) someone who was blown up in the First World War |
| **Floret:** | Eliot said this figure was 'entirely imaginary', but perhaps suggestive of 'folklore memories'. He is reminiscent of the legendary Actaeon (see note on 'running stags' above) and the god Attis in ancient fertility myths, killed by a wild boar, as was Adonis, who turned into a flower (Latin *floret*, he flowers): the connection with the cycle of death and rebirth seems clear, at any rate |
| **Pray . . . birth:** | the change from the expected concluding 'death' in this prayer (see *Ash-Wednesday* I) points to both the soul's birth into the new life and the need for prayer at the other beginning of the soul's journey, ordinary birth, before the child's life is corrupted in the ways the poem has shown |

## Marina (1930)

SUMMARY: A father meditates in wonderment on his daughter.

COMMENTARY: The title and the epigraph react against one another, effecting what Eliot described as a 'crisscross': the revealed truth in Shakespeare's play is wonderful; in contrast, the revealed truth in Seneca's is horrific. Each acts as a comment on the other, and a balanced tension results—especially when the Senecan rhetoric is then taken up in the first line of the poem, presenting a living child, not a slaughtered one.

This, the most touching and emotional of all the *Selected Poems*, uses the most powerfully affecting images and rhythms to parallel the wondering feelings of the father who is the speaker. Reservations are sometimes felt about the distinct tone of the 'Death' chant, but those ugly thumps dissolve miraculously into the wavelike return of pine and wood-thrush and fog.

The liturgical note of all the other poems of this period is absent, but 'grace' is truly here, and we notice the development of the sea and ships imagery of Part IV of *Ash-Wednesday*. Though the ship approaching the granite islands of the new world may be old and leaking, the victory over death is positive; even to 'Resign' life this time brings a totally positive anticipation of the new life, 'the hope, the new ships'. The images merge and regather in the overwhelming final cadences, until the breathed 'My daughter' fades out the sublime music. The least superficially religious poem of this period has become, at a deeper level, the most so.

NOTES AND GLOSSARY:

**title:** the daughter of Pericles, in Shakespeare's *Pericles*. She is associated with the sea because she was born at sea (*marina* is the Latin feminine adjective for 'marine', 'of the sea'): sea imagery is appropriately central to the poem also. In the play, the grown Marina, believed by her father to be long dead, is restored to him in what seems to him a miracle: this 'recognition' scene (V.1) Eliot considered one of the finest moments in literature

**epigraph:** the words of Hercules as he comes out of the madness in which he killed his wife and children ('What place is this, what region, what part of the world?') in the tragedy *Hercules Furens* (line 1138) by Seneca (*c.*4BC–AD65)

**Those who sharpen . . . :** a series of 'Death' images follows: those who use weapons; the vain; the complacent; the sexual. The animal images seem presented as a conflation of the Seven Deadly Sins: Anger and Envy (in the violent); Ambition and Pride (in the glittering); Sloth and Greed (in the pig-sty dwellers); and Lust (in the ecstatic)

**dog:** always evil and fearsome in Eliot (see 'Sweeney Among the Nightingales' and the boarhound in *Animula*)

**woodsong:** associates the song of the wood-thrush with its habitat

**What is this face . . . pulse:** recalls the bemused questions of Pericles: 'But are you flesh and blood?/Have you a working pulse . . .' (*Pericles* V.1)

**Given or lent:** echoes 'Given, not lent', a line by Alice Meynell (1847–1922) in her poem 'Unto Us a Son is Given', referring to Christ (the biblical prophecy of Isaiah 9:6)

**stars . . . eye . . . :** an image of transcendence ('beyond-ness') coexisting with an image of immanence ('within-ness')

**Whispers . . . leaves:** the image of hidden children recurs in Eliot; he may have derived it from Kipling's story 'They', in which ghostly children frolic about a blind woman's house

**I made this . . . :** this section points to the relationships between himself and vessel, vessel and daughter, himself and daughter; both his creations are contrasts, yet both are 'vessels' of redemption

**June . . . September:** in so far as this refers to the birth of his daughter, the September must fall in 'another' year to give nine months between conception and birth

**garboard strake:** first range of planks next to the keel in the bottom of a boat

## Choruses from 'The Rock' (1934)

*The Rock*, a pageant-play, was written for a church fund-raising campaign in London. Eliot provided some of the prose dialogue in this largely unimpressive work, but the verse choruses were his major contribution, and the only parts that he thought worth preserving. For *Selected Poems* he chose six of the ten choruses.

The pageant is about the building of a church, and particularly about the difficulties of building the Invisible Church in the modern world.

### Chorus I

SUMMARY: The need of the modern world for the Church.

COMMENTARY: The Chorus itself, as in classical Greek drama, is primarily there to provide a commentary on the action.

The biblical language, with many images and phrases and cadences drawn from the Bible (some of which are noted), is fundamental to the whole of *The Rock*, but it is mixed with ordinary colloquial speech to give an up-to-date yet timeless feel to the verse. Look, for instance, at the 'desert' chant, where the modern 'tube-train' sits next to the eternal 'heart of your brother'.

As you read on through the following Choruses, look out for changes in the verse when the Chorus changes emotional direction, as from pleading to anger, or meditative calm to ecstatic joy.

NOTES AND GLOSSARY:

**Eagle . . . Hunter:** these constellations are here used mainly to introduce the endless cycles of creation, hence the choice of ones whose names stress movement ('soars', 'pursues')

**the Word:** of God

**twenty centuries:** since Christ

**Dust:** as God told Adam, 'dust thou art, and unto dust shalt thou return'; see the Bible, Genesis 3:19

**timekept City:** financial area of London, ruled by the need for time-keeping (London has many church clocks with bells), as are its office workers

**foreign flotations:** pun on (*a*) overseas ships and (*b*) loans for overseas businesses (London was then the centre of world trade)

**chop-houses:** restaurants with cheap, ready-prepared food (useful for hurried businessmen)

**six days, on the seventh:** part of a parody of the religious observance of the sabbath (from God's rest on the seventh day of creation: Genesis 2:2–3)

**Hindhead . . . Maidenhead:** beauty spots near London

**papers:** the Sunday newspapers

**weddings:** in a secular age, weddings in church are still popular

**The Rock:** he is revealed at the end as Saint Peter (Christ's 'this rock': see 'The Hippopotamus'), but represents in a more general way those disciples who suffer for faith, bear witness to the Word, criticise the worldly, and so on. The whole 'rock' image relates also to God as a support, a frequent biblical usage, as in 2 Samuel 22:2: 'The Lord is my rock'

**I have trodden the winepress alone:** from Isaiah 63:3: the biblical metaphor of treading on grapes (to make juice for wine) is used for those who follow the orders (often angry) of God

*Make perfect your will:* to serve God, a biblical instruction Eliot may have come to via Dante's *Heaven* XXXIII, 103–5

**take no thought:** as in Matthew 6:34: 'Take therefore no thought for the morrow'

**Good and Evil:** for Eliot a clearcut and vital distinction (see Introduction); but compare Chorus X

**squeezed . . . tube-train:** London Underground trains are packed at rush hours

**the Unemployed:** of whom there were millions in the Depression of the 1930s

**No man has hired us:** the words of the unemployed labourers in Matthew 20:7

**In this land . . . :** begins a parody of God's promise of a prosperous land for the faithful, as in the Bible; see Jeremiah 32:41, 43

**'The Times':** where the deaths of the more 'important' are recorded

**shortened bed . . . narrow sheet:** adapted from the Bible, Isaiah 28:20

## Chorus II

SUMMARY: The need for the Church to be always building.

COMMENTARY: The long sentences in this Chorus are closer to prose than poetry: the feeling is that we are listening to the exhortations of a sermon.

NOTES AND GLOSSARY:

**Christ . . . cornerstone:** traditional development of Psalm 118: 'The stone which the builders refused has become the head stone of the corner'

**Spirit . . . waters:** as in Genesis 1:2, at the creation

**tortoise:** perhaps a reference to a Hindu creation myth in which the world is on the tortoise's back

**love our neighbour:** a central requirement of Christians, as in Matthew 19:19 (citing Leviticus 19:18): 'love thy neighbour as thyself'

**citizenship . . . Heaven:** as in 'fellow-citizens with the saints, and of the household of God' (see the Bible, Ephesians 2:19)

**Whipsnade:** a zoo near London

**imperial expansion:** an account of the British Empire follows

**prosperity . . . adversity:** opposites used, for example, in the Book of Common Prayer ('both in prosperity and adversity')

**ribbon roads:** with 'ribbons' of houses on either side, as around London in the 1920s and 1930s

## Chorus III

SUMMARY: A denunciation of Godless modern lives.

COMMENTARY: This Chorus is an imitation of the way the prophets in the Bible bring 'the Word of the Lord' to an erring people. Notice the emphatic questions and repetitions throughout.

NOTES AND GLOSSARY:

**designing:** (*a*) planning; (*b*) crafty

**enlightened:** as in the Age of Reason, or Enlightenment, rational thought may bring rejection of the spiritual

**race reports:** in newspapers, providing information for those who bet on races

**East:** the East End of London, with its dockland slums

**goat:** part of a prophecy, not a description

**North . . . West . . . South:** the wealthier middle-class areas outside London, later in the poem characterised by their gardens, tennis and golf

**build in vain ... keep the City:** as in the opening of Psalm 127: 'Except
the Lord build the house, they labour in vain that
build it: except the Lord keep the city, the watch-
man waketh but in vain'

**cavies:** guinea pigs (rodents)

**marmots:** squirrels (rodents)

**I have loved ...:** echoes Psalm 26: 'Lord, I have loved the habitation
of thy house'

**House:** of God (traditional way of referring to temple or
church)

**the Stranger:** one of the titles of 'The Rock' in the first Chorus;
later associated with Death

**common and preferred:** the stars anciently indicate men's fortune;
modern men seek another fortune on the stock
exchange in ordinary or preference shares

---

**Chorus VII**

---

SUMMARY: Religious history from the creation and through Christ to
the present gods.

COMMENTARY: A vast stretch of history is here compressed into the four
sections of poetic prose (Creation; Higher Religions; Christ; Atheism)
before the fragments of speech of the unemployed underline the 'waste
and void' lamented by the Chorus, in an age when the Church is not
regarded and unspiritual gods flourish.

NOTES AND GLOSSARY:
**In the beginning ... void ... deep:** from the account of creation in
Genesis 1:1-2

**Higher Religions:** as of the Jews and Muslims

**knowledge of Good and Evil:** a development into something good (for
Eliot: but see also Chorus X) of the forbidden 'tree
of the knowledge of good and evil' in Genesis 2:17

**Prayer wheels:** used especially by Tibetan Buddhists

**worship of the dead:** as in many primitive societies

**A moment:** the birth of Christ, where eternity cuts into time

**Passion:** of Christ, from the garden of Gethsemane to the
hill of Calvary

**Sacrifice:** of the Son of God on the Cross

**no god:** modern atheism

**Reason:** as in the eighteenth-century Enlightenment, the
intellectual movement putting its faith in rational
understanding as the means of obtaining knowledge and happiness

| Race: | belief in racial superiorities (Hitler came to power the previous year, 1933) |
| Dialectic: | an ideology based on opposed social forces, as in Marxism |

## Chorus IX

SUMMARY: A plea for all man's creative gifts to be used in the service of the Church.

COMMENTARY: Of the four creative gifts specified in the second section (sculpture, painting, music and word-making) it is the last that is particularly relevant and interesting to the poet: out of 'verbal imprecisions' he is here striving for a 'perfect order' of words and the beauty of singing speech—the incantation of the Choruses themselves. Now Eliot does not deny the senses, and, as the symbolic church is completed by religious adornments, the light imagery that dominates the final Chorus breaks in.

NOTES AND GLOSSARY:

**Son . . . :** the first three lines are entirely constructed from biblical phrases

**House . . . Sorrow:** a variation of Matthew 21:13 ('My house shall be called the house of prayer') to begin a description of the atmosphere in a typical church, contrasted with other public behaviour

**communion of saints:** a phrase from the Apostles' Creed in the Book of Common Prayer

**gifts to Your service:** a variation of the grace, 'Bless, O Lord, these gifts to our use and us to Thy service'

**Visible and invisible:** a phrase from the Nicene Creed, applied here to man's dual (physical and spiritual) nature

## Chorus X

SUMMARY: The built church, a light against evil darkness, is praised.

COMMENTARY: In the light imagery of this concluding Chorus, the poet is not only using traditional biblical associations but imitating Dante in the final Canto of *Paradise*, of which Eliot remarked: 'Nowhere in poetry has experience so remote from ordinary experience been expressed so concretely, by a masterly use of that imagery of *light* which is the form of certain types of mystical experience.' By his imitation, Eliot has also used concrete visual images of a large range of types of light to suggest the spiritual, Invisible Light.

NOTES AND GLOSSARY:

**light set on a hill:** a contraction of Christ's words in Matthew 5:14: 'Ye are the light of the world. A city that is set on a hill cannot be hid'

**great snake:** the Devil, as in the traditional development of the serpent in Genesis 3

**Iniquity:** of that same Satan, whose ways the people are warned against probing too deeply

**Good and Evil:** unlike in Chorus VII, suggesting the possible dangers of this knowledge if carried too far

**O Light Invisible, we praise Thee!:** echoes 'O World invisible, we view thee', the opening of 'The Kingdom of God', by Francis Thompson (1859–1907); God as the 'Light of Light' is praised in the Nicene Creed

**the less:** the lesser lights appear in the following lines: sunlight, moonlight, etcetera

**light of altar . . . sanctuary:** altar candles; and the light where the consecrated Host is reserved

**submarine:** as if looking from under water

**rocket:** at a fireworks display

**we give Thee . . . glory:** a version of a line in the Gloria, 'we give thanks to thee for thy great glory' (Book of Common Prayer)

# Part 3

# Commentary

## Borrowing and bettering

Anyone who looks through the notes in Part 2 can hardly help observing how much Eliot owes to others, whether it is the Laforguian *persona* he adopts in 'Prufrock' or the words about the Magi from Bishop Andrewes; whether it is the Dantean detail of *The Hollow Men* and *Ash-Wednesday* or the biblical phrases in the final Choruses . . . and so on. This may lead some readers to think less of Eliot, even to accuse him of stealing—an impression they may find reinforced when they discover whole books devoted to tracing his borrowings back to their sources.

Such an attitude would, however, be unjust to Eliot. It would unfairly deprive him of his due recognition as one of the most original poets ever to surprise the world. For Eliot transforms whatever he takes from others; he makes it distinctly his own. This is how he explained the process himself, in a defence of literary theft appropriately stolen from another critic, the French writer Rémy de Gourmont (1858–1915):

> One of the surest of tests is the way in which a poet borrows. Immature poets imitate; mature poets steal; bad poets deface what they take, and good poets make it into something better, or at least something different.

That is from the 1920 essay on the dramatist Philip Massinger (1583–1640). Thirty-six years later, in 'The Frontiers of Criticism', Eliot defined poetic originality as being largely 'an original way of assembling the most disparate and unlikely material to make a new whole'.

Readers should remember such remarks when considering any of the poems where an accusation of plagiarism seems valid. It will invariably be found, on closer inspection, that Eliot has either improved or at least changed the original—by applying it in a new context, by altering words to show the original in a new light, by reworking it for his own poetic purposes, and above all by recasting different borrowings in wholly new combinations that are entirely his own.

Let us take the example of Laforgue, who gave Eliot a significant early impetus. What we have here is not an example of a lesser poet following in the footsteps of a greater, but an example of a major poet learning from and developing the work of a comparatively minor one as part of his own development. As Eliot put it, he wanted to 'work out the implications of Laforgue' after a period in which the young poet was taken over by the 'stronger personality'—that is, the more forcefully individual poetic identity—of the Frenchman. Laforgue himself did not live long enough to follow up his 'implications' in this way, and it has been pointed out, but perhaps not often enough, that Eliot cannot properly be called an imitator of Laforgue because he is, in the words of the American critic Edmund Wilson (1895–1972), a 'superior artist . . . more mature than Laforgue ever was',* with a 'perfect' workmanship that Laforgue rarely approached. Eliot's achievement was to take hints from Laforgue and turn them, with a sure mastery that is beyond Laforgue's capabilities, into images and rhythms that have become embedded in the minds of all who read modern poetry. Far from speaking with another's voice, he has found for himself a poetic voice that is totally distinct, totally original: as F.R. Leavis put it, to learn from Laforgue in the way that Eliot did 'is to be original to the point of genius'.†

Much the same can be said even of Eliot's borrowings from Dante. For though that poet is, unlike Laforgue, not a lesser figure than Eliot himself, but a greater (as we have seen, Eliot put him on a level with Shakespeare), the use Eliot made of the Italian was also decisively directed towards his own unique vision—though 'decisively' seems the wrong word to use of a vision as tentative and exploratory as Eliot's spiritual search in the later poems; his modern hesitancy is in this way very different from Dante's medieval certainty, and no less poetically effective for that.

In short, Eliot knew exactly how to 'Make it New'. The 'it' might have been something found elsewhere: after all, literature is always concerned with many of the permanent subjects of human interest, such as time, love, reality and all the rest, crudely summed up by Sweeney (in the unfinished *Sweeney Agonistes*) as 'Birth, and copulation, and death'. An 'it' from any such central human topics is bound to have been treated countless times before. But Eliot used his genius to find a new angle, a new atmosphere, a new image or combination of images, a whole new poetic language to say things afresh.

This is one reason why a continual chasing after sources has its dangers, and why it must be stressed that explanatory notes of the kind found in Part 2 are not only no substitute for a reading of the poems themselves, but are also only first steps towards an understanding of the poems *as poetry*—as opposed to certain types of factual prose that have a definable, limited, objective, unambiguous meaning. As Eliot once said, the explanation of literary works must not be mistaken for the

*'T.S. Eliot', *Axel's Castle*, Fontana Paperbacks, Collins, London, 1961, p.85.
†In *New Bearings in English Poetry*, Penguin Books, Harmondsworth, 1963, p.69.

understanding of such works: the idea that once a poem (or a novel, or a play) has been 'explained' then that is all we need to bother about. It is, of course, only the start of our response, and sometimes perhaps not even that: Eliot believed that we can respond to the poetry before we know very much about what the poem 'means'. What we do not want is to be left clutching the explanation alone, while the poetry has flown out of our grasp.

As an illustration, let us see how Eliot can both use a particular echo of another writer and make it into such a new thing that to track down the source is only one way of heading towards what the reader's most basic response needs to be. A note in Part 2 on the final line of 'Sweeney Among the Nightingales'—'To stain the stiff dishonoured shroud'— may well have pointed out the echo of 'dim/Dishonoured brow', from 'Ichabod' (translates 'the glory has departed'), a poem by John Green-leaf Whittier (1807–92) about the American politician Daniel Webster (1782–1852), which supports the theme of betrayal already presented in the murder of Agamemnon, and paralleled by the intrigue against Sweeney. This sort of information can be helpful to the reader, if only by indicating certain reinforcing themes that could be followed up. But it is obvious that the essence of the line can only be extracted by reference to both the context of the line and its own impact, with the alliterated hissing sounds, and particularly the repeated 'st', imitating the bird droppings splattering on the sheet covering the dead man, where they probably add to the stiffness already caused by his dried blood and *rigor mortis*—and certainly add, even if only figuratively, to the dishonour of that death, which has in turn led some critics to see a connection with sleepy Sweeney and suggest a 'wet dream' as the source of his dishonourable stain . . . Where does one stop? Some interpretations have to be ruled out, as a line that means anything and everything is meaningless. But this cannot alter the fact that no source-citing is going to exhaust such a line of its possible resonances; nor can it account for the new impact, in a new context, of such borrowings, whether they are better or only different.

The transformation of Eliot's borrowings may be found early and late, if perhaps less dramatically in the later verse than in the earlier. It may be useful to glance now at these 'early' and 'late' classifications, and how they affect our view of Eliot's development.

## Pre-conversion and post-conversion

This is a favourite way of dividing the poetry into what was published before and what was published after Eliot's reception into the Church of England. The works dating from beyond the end of *Selected Poems* (*Four Quartets* and the poetic dramas) fall into the second category, as does everything in *Selected Poems* after *The Hollow Men*, which is a kind of borderline marker.

In obvious ways, this distinction is true enough, and a helpful way of remembering certain characteristic differences between the two groups it forms. Even critics who insist most strongly on the underlying unity of Eliot's entire output have to face the fact that the man who wrote *Four Quartets* was a Christian and the man who wrote *The Waste Land* was not; that the lampooner of the Church in 'The Hippopotamus' was later to support it in his contributions to *The Rock*; that the satirist who mocked church wordiness in 'Mr Eliot's Sunday Morning Service' took church words reverently into 'A Song for Simeon'. What is more, the poet's later style—or perhaps one should say range of styles, for he never exactly repeated himself—is recognisably different from the earlier, so much so that many former admirers became critical and many of the formerly hostile became approving. In the same way, the overtly Christian themes indicated by titles such as *Ash-Wednesday* or *Journey of the Magi* converted some Christians into readers of Eliot, just as they turned away unbelieving former readers who had found his earlier view of the world more to their taste.

All the same, two opposite things must be remembered about Eliot's work that the 'early' versus 'late', 'pre-conversion' versus 'post-conversion' division does not take into account: on the one hand, that there are more possible divisions than this; on the other, that Eliot progresses in a single curve as each new work evolves from what has gone before. There are further sub-divisions, within the 'early' poems particularly, which are easily illustrated: look, for example, at the difference between the 'free' poems in *Prufrock and Other Observations* and the strict quatrains in *Poems 1920*. Eliot's evolving development is less easy to illustrate briefly, but some idea of it may be got from various approaches: following through the metamorphoses of Eliot's characteristic voices and *personae* from, say, Prufrock to Gerontion, Gerontion to Simeon; or noticing how 'Gerontion', for instance, was originally to be part of *The Waste Land*, bits left over from which in turn developed into *The Hollow Men*; or even looking back from the achieved vision in the later poems of acceptance to see how it had its origin in the implied quest for an alternative in the earlier poems of rejection.

# Prosody and punctuation

Eliot's mastery of versification shows itself in the variety of verse forms to which he successfully turned his hand at different times. He exploits the possibilities of a form with considerable daring. For instance, even in his quatrain poems, with their given rhymes and rhythms, he breaks out of the form now and then to run over from one usually self-contained four-lined stanza into another. The two 'declinings' in 'Burbank . . .' are illustrations of this:

> The smoky candle end of time
> Declines. . .
> She entertains Sir Ferdinand
> Klein.

The high culture of the Canaletto and Mantegna paintings falls off sadly into the low modern civilisation represented by Bleistein; the acquired grandeur of the now titled upstart falls down ludicrously at his delayed 'small' surname: it is all done by the versification. Another technique in the regularly rhymed poems is to use the compulsory rhymes themselves to make a point, as in the deliberately pathetic rhyme-words used in 'A Cooking Egg', where 'Sidney' collapses to 'kidney', or the 'trumpets', in a more tragic context, sink to 'crumpets'.

But even in his so-called 'free' verse, Eliot makes use of such devices, including rhyme. For 'free verse', in Eliot, does not mean that rhyme is totally abandoned. On the contrary, Eliot saw that an irregular rhyme could be used—to greater effect than in much regularly rhymed verse— in a poem with a 'free' structure 'where rhyme is wanted for some special effect, for a sudden tightening-up, for a cumulative insistence, or for an abrupt change of mood' ('Reflections on *Vers Libre*'). An example of a sudden tightening-up would be the end of 'Rhapsody on a Windy Night', where the aimless unrhymed detail of remembered routine is caught up by the constriction of the final cruel rhyme, itself also a 'last twist':

> '. . . The little lamp spreads a ring on the stair.
> Mount.
> The bed is open; the tooth-brush hangs on the wall,
> Put your shoes at the door, sleep, prepare for life.'
>
> The last twist of the knife.

A cumulative insistence is usually achieved in Eliot's work by repeated words and phrases rather than rhymes, but in a passage like Part III of *Ash-Wednesday* the 'stair' rhymes and echoes mount with the ascending of the staircase: stair, (banister), air, (stairs . . . wears), despair, stair, repair, stair, (hair . . . hair), hair, stair, despair, stair. An abrupt change of mood is effected by the banal rhyme in 'Prufrock' where, after an ominous scene setting, we get the trivial ding-dong of

> In the room the women come and go
> Talking of Michelangelo.

However, 'Prufrock' has more rhymed than unrhymed lines, and it often happens in such poems that an *un*rhymed line signals a change, as in the striking interruption of 'No! I am not Prince Hamlet . . .' after (floor-more; mean-screen; shawl-all . . .) and before (do-two; tool-Fool . . .) a series of rhymes, or as in the switch of mood at the final three unrhymed lines of the rhyming 'Preludes'.

It is remarkable how much, not how little, rhyme is used in *Selected Poems*. There are only two works in the whole book that do not at some stage use end-rhymes, 'Gerontion' and 'Journey of the Magi', the two works prominently using the prose sermons of Bishop Andrewes as stepping stones. ('Gerontion' also prominently uses other prose borrowings and imitates the unrhymed blank verse of the Jacobean dramatists.) Of course there are large unrhymed sections in the other works, particularly later, but all the others use rhyme at some stage. Even the almost totally unrhymed final Choruses break into rhyme now and then, as at the end of Chorus I (build-tilled, bread-bed . . .) or the internal rhymes of 'What does the world say, does the world stray in high-powered cars on a by-pass way?' in Chorus VII. Yet the verse given to Gerontion and the Magus is just as 'poetic' in each case as it is anywhere else and uses many of the same techniques. 'Gerontion', for instance, employs assonances and alliterations that have much of the echoing and welding effect of full rhyme: 'Blistered in Brussels, patched and peeled . . .'; 'The woman keeps the kitchen, makes tea, / Sneezes at evening, poking the peevish . . .'. And 'Journey of the Magi' uses Eliot's characteristic later device of words repeated again and again as in chanting, whether these are the significant words of the theme (birth, death) or normally unimportant words like the 'and' that rhetorically piles up the Magi's problems:

> Then the camel men cursing and grumbling
> And running away, and wanting their liquor and women,
> And the night-fires going out, and the lack of shelters,
> And the cities hostile and the towns unfriendly
> And the villages dirty and charging high prices.

That last quotation is also useful as an illustration of the fact that, as Eliot said, 'scansion tells us very little'. Determined efforts have been made by various critics to scan Eliot's verse, with diagrams showing where light syllables alternate with stressed ones, and those who care to do so can mark and count up the beats and the feet in any line they choose—but the usefulness of such exercises is, unfortunately, very limited. In the lines quoted, as everywhere else, any prosodic interest arises out of the variations from an underlying norm. Even if one does not know that, say, it is the departure from the prevailing two-syllable 'iambs' (unstressed followed by stressed syllable) to the galloping three-syllable 'anapaests' (two unstressed syllables followed by a stressed one) that helps the mounting effect of problem after problem, one can observe such an effect—it helps to read aloud—without having to rely on complicated and dubious prosodic jargon.

It is the same with rhymed lines: the metrical interest comes from variation. Look how the second or rhyming lines have a different number of syllables from the first, sometimes only slightly different, sometimes prominently so, in the following passage from *Ash-Wednesday*:

> And the lost heart stiffens and rejoices
> In the lost lilac and the lost sea voices
> And the weak spirit quickens to rebel
> For the bent golden-rod and the lost sea smell
> Quickens to recover
> The cry of quail and the whirling plover . . .

We seem to be always on the verge of a steady rhythmic pattern, yet always the carpet is pulled from under our feet, jerking us into awareness. Eliot is following his own dictum that:

> the most interesting verse which has yet been written in our language has been done either by taking a very simple form, like the iambic pentameter, and constantly withdrawing from it, or taking no form at all, and constantly approximating to a very simple one. It is this contrast between fixity and flux, this unperceived evasion of monotony, which is the very life of verse.

Applying these observations to the poems will be found of great value to the student of Eliot's prosody. It needs no special knowledge, only an ear sensitive to rhythm.

Another of Eliot's dicta is that verse, whatever else it is, is 'a system of punctuation'. Despite the concern he shows here, Eliot's practice has not always been thought to be as careful as it might have been. Look at that passage quoted from *Ash-Wednesday* to find a momentary confusion about whether it is the spirit or the smell that 'Quickens to recover'. It is useful to remember that Eliot thought final commas were often unnecessary, as he himself always paused slightly at the end of a line of verse, but this does not help readers to see at once where the sense of a line runs on (as after 'rebel') and where it evidently breaks (as after 'smell'). There is a more serious instance in the same poem:

> And I pray that I may forget
> These mattters that with myself I too much discuss
> Too much explain
> Because I do not hope to turn again
> Let these words answer
> For what is done, not to be done again
> May the judgment not be too heavy upon us . . .

The lack of punctuation at the ends of the lines has here made it uncertain whether the 'Because . . .' line goes with what precedes or follows it, or whether the 'For what is done' line completes the sense of the 'answer' in the previous line or leads on to 'May the judgment'. Readers have to decide the punctuation for themselves, and it makes a difference whether they choose to put something like a full stop after 'turn again', or after 'answer', or after 'done again'.

Nor is punctuational confusion limited to the later, often lightly punctuated poems. There is a famous instance in the third stanza of 'Whispers of Immortality', which varies in punctuation from edition to edition: nothing after 'sense' and a comma after 'penetrate'; a semicolon after 'sense' and a comma after 'penetrate'; a comma after 'sense' and a semicolon after 'penetrate'. It is a useful exercise to see what effect on the meaning each change has. And, despite the irritation that some may feel, it is perhaps amusing that readers may accept the latest (third) punctuation as the most authoritative, or prefer an earlier one, or even suggest a fourth non-existent version (nothing after 'sense' and a semicolon after 'penetrate' might be the clearest) as the 'best' reading.

The developments in Eliot's prosody and punctuation from early to late are all part of larger developments, so it seems appropriate to set them in the following larger contexts.

## Styles and structures

It has been pointed out that when one is looking for illustrations of different poetic styles, the most obvious thing is to set any other of Eliot's works against the controversial and influential quatrain poems, with their strict forms, their brilliant verbal wit, their sophistication, their frequently learned, ingenious, ironic, fantastical, superior, detached or unfeeling effects and tones. They are quite different from anything else, and so are convenient to employ in critical contrasts—provided one does not forget the contrasts also possible within this group, or even within individual poems, as in the extraordinary changes of mood in 'A Cooking Egg' (and its extraordinary extra line) and in 'Sweeney Among the Nightingales'.

What is not so simple to show, and what has indeed never been very clearly shown, is the complex of differences between other poems from different periods. The crucial reason for this is that every time a distinction is made, an awareness of an essential similarity makes itself felt. In the same way, every time a similarity is asserted, an unignorable difference inconveniently raises its head. All the poetry bears the unmistakable imprint of a single poetic sensibility; at the same time, this poet never exactly repeated a poetic voice or manner that he had used earlier. So what we must aim at is a kind of double vision that can note differences in different periods and poems, while keeping an eye open for similarities.

Thus, Eliot is at his best in all periods when he is in some way dramatic. There is no poem in *Selected Poems* that does not in some way dramatise a situation or a mood. Even the most inward states exploit essentially dramatic external situations, as do the thinking voices from 'Prufrock', through 'Gerontion' and *The Hollow Men*, to the final *Choruses*; even the most abstract concepts are given concrete life, as in the spiritual progress dramatised on the stairs in Part III of *Ash-Wednesday*, or the spiritual regression dramatised in the childhood scenes of 'Animula'.

At the same time Eliot's startling earlier poems are more dramatic than lyrical, and his less startling later poems are more lyrical and meditative than dramatic. The difference can be seen by comparing, say,

> Now that lilacs are in bloom
> She has a bowl of lilacs in her room
> And twists one in her fingers while she talks.
> 'Ah, my friend, you do not know, you do not know
> What life is, you who hold it in your hands';
> (Slowly twisting the lilac stalks)
> 'You let it flow from you, you let it flow,
> And youth is cruel, and has no remorse
> And smiles at situations which it cannot see.'
> I smile, of course,
> And go on drinking tea . . .

and

> Blown hair is sweet, brown hair over the mouth blown,
> Lilac and brown hair;
> Distraction, music of the flute, stops and steps of the mind over the
>     third stair,
> Fading, fading; strength beyond hope and despair
> Climbing the third stair.

There are remarkable similarities here, from the characteristically regretful use of lilac to the rhymes at the end of lines of varying length. But the repetitions in 'Portrait of a Lady' are not used to the same end as the repetitions in *Ash-Wednesday*: 'you do not know, you do not know' is not a foreshadowing of, but in another poetic world from, 'Because I do not hope to know . . . Because I know I shall not know'— for the simple reason that the lady's affectedness is being mocked, while the twistings and turnings of the convert are anything but mocked. Her sexual longings are made pathetic; his are felt with tragic intensity. In the first case the repetitions underline what is pitiable and contribute humorous satirical exaggeration; in the other the repetitions provide a lyrical note of yearning that is purely sympathetic. And of course nowhere in *Ash-Wednesday* is there anything remotely like the casually cruel demolition job of

> I smile, of course,
> And go on drinking tea . . .

Then there is versification. Eliot uses a number of different types throughout, but the greatest variety is found in the earlier work. There we have the rhymed speech-rhythm, the unstressed unwindings of 'Prufrock' ('Let us go then, you and I,/When the evening is spread out against the sky . . .') or the 'Portrait'—

> The October night comes down; returning as before
> Except for a slight sensation of being ill at ease
> I mount the stairs and turn the handle of the door
> And feel as if I had mounted on my hands and knees.

—immediately followed by the rhymed beat-rhythm, the stressed definition of 'Preludes':

> His soul stretched tight across the skies
> That fade behind a city block,
> Or trampled by insistent feet
> At four and five and six o'clock . . .

Or we can contrast the unrhymed blank verse effects of 'Gerontion' with the regularly rhymed 'fixed' structures following it in *Selected Poems*, or with the irregularly rhymed 'organic' structures which precede it.

The differences are more striking than the similarities in these early works, culminating in *The Waste Land*. When we turn to the later works, however, the similarities are more noticeable than the differences. Even what look at first sight like obvious changes of direction within a poem usually turn out to be sharing the same tempo and mood as the rest, as when Eliot's version of the Litany of the Virgin Mary ('Lady of silences'), with its short lines on the page, is essentially close to the endlessly circling lines of the rest of *Ash-Wednesday*: 'End of the endless/Journey to no end/Conclusion of all that/Is inconclusible/Speech without word and/Word of no speech' is more like than unlike 'Against the Word the unstilled world still whirled/About the centre of the silent Word'.

There is a feeling that the characteristic later verse forms have taken Eliot right out of the reach of conventional prosody: earlier one feels he is reacting against established forms by twisting them into new shapes; later one feels he is creating his own forms, following his own rules rather than breaking the rules of others. It is largely a matter of the prevailing rhythm.

Again, Eliot in all periods displays great rhythmic variety, both from poem to poem and within individual poems. But his rhythms are typically more varied and energetic before *The Hollow Men*, and more relaxed and repetitious after that. The greatest range of rhythmic vitality and variation will be found in *The Waste Land*, but almost any other section of the earlier work provides more of this range than can be found in the later. The early range includes such juxtapositions as incantatory, prophet-in-the-wilderness Prufrock letting his biblical rhetoric fall through swift rhythmic gradations to self-deprecatory, please-don't-bother Prufrock of the easy-going phrase:

> But though I have wept and fasted, wept and prayed,
> Though I have seen my head (grown slightly bald) brought in upon
>   a platter,
> I am no prophet—and here's no great matter . . .

It also includes such combinations as the excited entrance of Sir Ferdinand moving ambiguously to the melancholy meditations of Burbank:

> Lights, lights,
> She entertains Sir Ferdinand
> Klein. Who clipped the lion's wings
>   And flea'd his rump and pared his claws?
> Thought Burbank, meditating on
>   Time's ruins, and the seven laws.

The later poems do not characteristically exhibit this kind of rapid shifting. This is not to say the later poems are less good, only that their characteristic method is different. This method uses incantatory rhythms that repeat over and again the words and phrases that the poet is meditatively exploring:

> If the lost word is lost, if the spent word is spent
> If the unheard, unspoken
> Word is unspoken, unheard;
> Still is the unspoken word, the Word unheard,
> The Word without a word . . .

This is the opposite of the early verse, where the speed and complexity of the changes, with the associated concision, demand great alertness on the part of the reader. Here, we find instead an expansion and general loosening-up.

This loosening-up is seen in the structures of the later verse, in both the smaller and the larger units. In the case of the larger units of complete poems, Eliot's method of composition, joining up bits to form

new wholes, seems to have contributed to the impression of occasion-
ally over-extended conglomerations. This is perhaps more noticeable
in the later poems, where some assemblages, despite all the similarities
of tone and texture, seem to lack the earlier air of tightly-knit inevitability, despite all the variety. It may be relevant to note that poems
like 'Prufrock' and *The Waste Land* were reduced to their present form
from larger structures, whereas poems like *The Hollow Men* and *Ash-
Wednesday* grew from shorter, separate structures. Certainly, in the
smaller units of phrases, sentences and paragraphs, we find the economy
and urgency of lines like

> The tiger springs in the new year. Us he devours.
>     Think at last
> We have not reached conclusion, when I
> Stiffen in a rented house . . .

largely abandoned for the less concentrated, gentler flux and reflux
of thought:

> Will the veiled sister pray for
> Those who walk in darkness, who chose thee
>     and oppose thee . . .?
>         Will the veiled sister pray
> For children at the gate
> Who will not go away and cannot pray:
> Pray for those who chose and oppose[?]

The repetitive, looser quality of the later poems is mirrored by their
characteristic imagery, which is vaguer, more dreamlike and beautiful
than the characteristically striking, realistic, precise earlier imagery.
Where the earlier style of writing brings off audacious feats with its
sordid city images and perpetually surprising combinations of words,
the later style turns to nature and almost always avoids upsetting the
prevailing mood of thoughtful deliberation by any very startling change
of direction in either imagery or sentence-structure. The personal
trademarks of street and suchlike images are left behind when the poet
adapts the images found in older traditions, such as the rose of medieval allegory, the Garden of Paradise, the biblical desert.

# Themes and variations

It is a rewarding exercise to go through Eliot's poetry looking for
recurrences of images and themes, noting any developments as well as
repetitions. Nothing else can more helpfully and easily bring out the
poet's enduring concerns and the overall links between each part of the
larger work formed by his total output. We are concerned here only

with *Selected Poems*, but the principle holds good for that whole, as well as the larger totality.

The images that recur are of many kinds. The American critic Leonard Unger* (*b.*1916) has made a useful list of some of the most prominent ones, and a list like this is an excellent place for the interested student to begin: flowers and gardens; water; times of year (months and seasons) and times of day; smoke and fog; city streets; human parts, including hair; stairs; music; smell.

*Flower* and *garden* images have been frequently pointed out, especially in Part 2 of these Notes. Notice particularly the spring flowers, hyacinth and lilac, at times of yearning remembrance, the use of trees, and the juxtaposition of garden images with *desert* ones. Whereas the *wasteland* images are barren, waiting for rain, the desert has a dual role: sterile, but a place of spiritual renewal. Remember that the evergreen yew, which began as a symbol of immortality, became associated with *death* by its constant use in graveyards: Eliot uses it in both ways. Other death images that can have dual associations are *bones*, as in *Ash-Wednesday*, though in the earlier poems bones are used mainly for their negative associations, emphasised by their frequent placing next to *rats* (as three times in *The Waste Land*). The groups of *animal* images (such as ape, fox, dog, cat—including tiger, jaguar and leopard) are used mainly for threatening effects, in poems as different as 'Sweeney Among the Nightingales' and 'Animula'. This will take us on to other creatures like *birds* . . . at which point, its range of possible additions having been demonstrated, our given list can be resumed.

The most striking *water* images, apart from the situations where water is lacking in the dry land and where the desiccated wait for an often spiritual rain, are the *sea* images, which occur at particularly moving moments of recollection and revelation in poems as various as 'Prufrock', 'Gerontion', 'Burbank . . .', *Ash-Wednesday* and 'Marina'.

*Times* of year and day are used for their emotional resonances so regularly that it is only in some of the quatrain poems that no examples will strike the attentive reader. Notice the use of the spring (April to May) not simply as a conventional image of joyous renewal but as a 'cruel' reminder; and the use of 'twilight', intermediate times of day, for uncertain, intermediate states. *Smoke* and *fog* are usually part of the complex of images from *city streets* and modern life generally, though there is a notably different use of fog in 'Marina'.

Arms, hands and fingers, legs and feet, heads and eyes are all examples of *human parts* used prominently by Eliot to stand for people and direct our feelings. Perhaps the most powerful of such images is the human hair, occurring in 'Prufrock', *The Waste Land*, and *Ash-Wednesday*.

*In 'T.S. Eliot's Images of Awareness', *T.S. Eliot: The Man and His Work*, ed. Allen Tate, Chatto & Windus, London, 1967, pp.205-6.

*Stairs* are chiefly associated with the sexually troubled, whether it is the narrator's worry about women at the top of the stairs ('Prufrock', 'Portrait'), or the lack of a woman ('Rhapsody'), or the loss of a woman ('Burbank . . .'), or a dead relationship with a woman (*The Waste Land*), or the renunciation of women (*Ash-Wednesday*). The climbing of stairs is therefore difficult, morally and emotionally, even for the saints who mount their symbolic stair in 'A Song for Simeon'.

Eliot's interest in *music* is seen in such titles as 'Preludes', 'Rhapsody on a Windy Night', 'A Song for Simeon', and *Four Quartets*, where this interest culminates. 'Portrait of a Lady' uses musical motifs throughout, and lesser instances may be found in many other poems.

Finally, the use of *smell* is an enduring characteristic of Eliot's imagery, from all those early (and especially female) smells, encountered in streets and drawing-rooms ('Rhapsody' has a long list), to the smells of flowers encountered early and late.

The imagery a poet uses is one way he gives life to his themes. The themes that Eliot explores in *Selected Poems* can be followed up by the student (with the help of Part 2, as needed) in much the same way as the imagery can be, and at the same time. For the types of images chosen by the poet will help in indicating aspects of his themes.

Typical themes in Eliot grow out of answering two related questions: How do we live? and How should we live? The answer to the first question predominates in the early poems, which typically examine the nature of the wasteland within individual modern lives and show how such lives are barely 'lived' at all: the theme of the unlived life, of timid withdrawal from life, is significant here. This early answer is a largely descriptive answer; it does not provide much in the way of alternatives to the prevailing sterility. The answer to the second question rises out of the first answer and predominates in the later poems, which typically examine the spiritual needs of the wastelanders and suggest what must be done to make the desert bloom: here the ascetic theme of renunciation, of dying to the old life to be born into the new, becomes important. Though this later answer is largely prescriptive, only at times in the final *Choruses* does the poetry smack of blatant religious propaganda: more usually, everything is too tentative and exploratory and wondering to be labelled didactic and exhortatory.

Some important themes are related to time. For example, *Selected Poems* plays many variations on the theme of the relationship of past to present, telling a story of decay by juxtaposing the glorious ancients and the inglorious moderns (as in Prufrock and Michelangelo or John the Baptist or Hamlet, the 'Lady' and Juliet, Burbank and Mark Antony, Sweeney's girl and Ariadne or Nausicaa), but also deromanticising figures from the past to show that their human frailty is essentially shared with ours (as in Agamemnon, the Roman legionaries, the Magi,

Simeon). Later in *Selected Poems* the significance of the birth of Christ (the Incarnation), a moment both in time and out of it (in eternity), is an important development of a 'time' theme that will be taken further in *Four Quartets*.

Other large themes that might be pursued through *Selected Poems* include: appearance and reality, the actual and the ideal, the quest, the nature of belief, suffering, salvation, good and evil, the links between art and life.

To conclude, here are three general observations about *Selected Poems* that point to both the enduring interests of the poet and the enduring interest that the poetry holds for readers, which is the final topic to be discussed. Firstly, there is the persistence in the memory, as in the poems, of certain characters like Sweeney; like his opposite, Prufrock (the 'Prufrockian' *persona* is adapted in several other characters, such as the narrator of 'Portrait', Gerontion, Burbank, the narrator of *The Hollow Men* and Simeon); like the sinister Jews; and like the women, who are often made to seem either rather repulsive at close quarters, or unattainably remote and idealised. Secondly, it is remarkable how personal Eliot's poetry is, despite all his insistence on the impersonality of art and on the strict need to separate the man who suffers from the mind which creates. He learnt from Laforgue how to utilise personal problems in poetry, and the special interest his poetry provides as a sort of autobiography of mental and spiritual breakdown and recovery is not at all easy to deny. Thirdly, only prudery could enable readers to ignore the fact that the personal theme that most persistently underlies Eliot's poetry is sexual: it may be intellectualised or disguised or impersonalised, but the erotic note, as sounded in frustration, disappointment, disgust, regret and longing, insistently recurs.

# The writer and his readers

Because of its frequent obscurity, its learnedness, its quotations and allusions, Eliot's poetry often seems to be deliberately elitist, seeking to appeal to an intellectual minority rather than a wide audience. But Eliot himself said this:

> I believe that the poet naturally prefers to write for as large and miscellaneous an audience as possible, and that it is the half-educated and ill-educated, rather than the uneducated, who stand in his way: I myself should like an audience which could neither read nor write.

This remark, from the conclusion to *The Use of Poetry and the Use of Criticism* (p.152), could hardly be further from a desire for a limited and highly literate audience of adepts. So, while it is true that Eliot is not a popular poet in the sense that he is read by a mass audience (more have

heard of *The Waste Land* than actually read it), the comparative small-
ness of his public may say more about his reputation as a 'difficult' poet
than about his potential appeal. And perhaps one should stress that
'comparative': by the standards of most poets, Eliot is read very widely
indeed, as the unflagging reprintings of his works testify.

A reputation for intellectual difficulty—and it is pointless to deny a
measure of difficulty in Eliot—is not the only block to a (still) wider
appeal. Criticism has also been levelled at the narrowness of Eliot's
interests, and particularly to a gap in his poetry that has been neatly
summed up by Grover Smith, who regretted that Eliot's poetry 'shows
no Beatrice'.* It has been further objected that there is so much that
is negative in this poetry, so much rejection, sterility and renunciation.

But such views, even if we share them, must not blind us to the
virtues of the poetry; nor must any intellectual emphasis, or Eliot's
rejection of certain romantic attitudes, or his protective mask of irony,
be allowed to oust from our minds a realisation of the fundamentally
emotional nature of this poetry. It betrays the romantic side of the
poet's temperament and the depths of feeling from which, with a voice
controlled by a critical intelligence, he speaks most powerfully and
memorably.

'A thorough knowledge of Eliot is compulsory for anyone interested
in contemporary literature. Whether he is liked or disliked is of no
importance, but he must be read.' Northrop Frye's words† are still
true, though some would wish to stress that the sense of the importance
of the poetry does not rule out enjoyment and excitement. The excitement was still there for Ezra Pound after his friend's death: 'I can only
repeat, but with the urgency of fifty years ago: READ HIM.'‡

---

*In *T.S. Eliot's Poetry and Plays*, University of Chicago Press, Chicago and London, revised edition, 1974, p.7.
†*T.S. Eliot*, Oliver & Boyd, Edinburgh and London, 1963, p.5.
‡'For TSE', *T.S. Eliot: The Man and His Work*, ed. Allen Tate, 1967, p.92.

## Part 4

# Hints for study

## Preliminary advice

A good dictionary, such as *The Concise Oxford Dictionary of Current English*, is a necessity for all students of literature. Use it to look up the meaning of every word that puzzles you; or to check that there are not other meanings that may be relevant; or to find out more about its origin. Literature exploits the connotations as well as the denotations of words, so the more you find out about particular words, the better placed you will be to discuss their literary effects. The dictionary not only helps with difficult words in your reading (such as 'connotations' and 'denotations', perhaps) but also helps in your own writing about that reading: you will not impress by using the wrong words, or spelling them wrongly, so use the dictionary to check.

You must become familiar with a good range of Eliot's poetry. The larger your chosen range the better, provided you do not sacrifice the deep and detailed knowledge of a few poems for a sketchy and superficial acquaintance with many poems. Aim at a balance: a reasonable number of poems, *not* all from the same period, that you know really well, and a probably larger number that you know less intimately, but can draw on for support in particular matters. It is best to concentrate on particular matters, by the way: the specific, cited instance tends to be more convincing than the vague, unsupported generalisation.

Your familiarity with the poems will probably need to be put to the test in your writing about them in essays, perhaps under examination conditions. You will want to prepare yourself as efficiently as possible by reading the poems, thinking about them, and practising writing about them. Try to make all these activities directed towards specific ends. For instance, after you have read a poem (or a section of a poem) for its general effect, and perhaps used the notes for elucidations and ideas, go back and read it again, looking out for striking images. Then read it again for the rhythm. And so on. At another stage, you could move between different poems, comparing and contrasting the things you have noticed (and preferably noted down in writing) in each separate poem. By such means, you will become so familiar with the poems that, when asked a question, you will think of a number of examples on which you can base your answer. The citing of examples is part of any answer because it shows your precise knowledge of the text and your ability to use the evidence to prove the points in your argument. For examination purposes, it is useful to be able to quote short passages from memory, but in any case you will always need to illustrate the points you are making by some close reference to the text.

The study of *Selected Poems* on its own is a perfectly possible and valid activity. But some students will want to turn also to Eliot's other poems, especially *Four Quartets*, the poetic dramas. All students will benefit from the study of Eliot's criticism: the theoretical counterpart of his poetic practice, it provides focal points for the study of the poems, as well as being valuable in its own right (see Part 5 of these Notes).

# Essay topics

One list of topics for study can be compiled by going through the notes in Part 2; another by going through Part 3 and turning some of the main points into questions, something like this:

(a) How original is Eliot? Is he a plagiarist? In what ways does he follow Pound's advice to 'Make it New'?

(b) What differences are there between Eliot's earlier and later poems? How would you describe the stages of Eliot's development?

(c) Is Eliot a master of versification? How fixed are his fixed forms, the quatrains? How free is his 'free verse'? In what ways does he use rhyme? And rhythm? Do you find his punctuation adequate?

(d) How would you illustrate the dramatic qualities of Eliot's verse? Is he more dramatic earlier? Does he show less vitality and variety later? Do the methods of the later poems have any advantages?

(e) What types of imagery are peculiar to the earlier poems? And what to the later? What examples would you choose of recurring images? And of recurring themes?

(f) In what ways is Eliot a 'difficult' poet? Do you find the pleasures compensate for the occasional problems? What do you make of Eliot's desire for an illiterate audience? What makes Eliot an important poet?

This kind of list is capable of great extension. Here is a selection of further typical topics to follow up in *Selected Poems*:

(1) State as fully as you can the meanings and associations you attach to the following: Prufrock; Sweeney; Grishkin; Pipit; lilacs and hyacinths; bones; yews; fog; hair; stairs; sea; light; eyes; rocks; wind; twilight; violet; the garden; the desert.

(2) What do the epigraphs to Eliot's poems contribute? And the titles?

(3) Describe some outstanding features of Eliot's use of the dramatic monologue.

(4) What is your reaction to Eliot's use of allusions to other works?

(5) Does Eliot's poetry strike you as primarily intellectual or emotional?

(6) Which poem means the most to you, and why?

(7) Do you agree that Eliot's poetry shows little affection for human life?

(8) Is there any humour in Eliot's poetry?

(9) 'Suffering is the underlying experience in all Eliot's poetry.' Do you agree?

(10) How far is Eliot a religious poet?

(11) Write a detailed critical analysis of any one poem, paying particular attention to such matters as the movement of the verse, the imagery and the tone.

(12) Write a detailed critical appreciation of any two or three poems so as to bring out the variety in Eliot's achievement.

(13) Illustrate Eliot's use of a *persona*.

(14) 'The Love Song of J. Alfred Prufrock' seemed disjointed and even 'insane' when first published. Can you refute such allegations by an analysis of the links in and development of the poem?

(15) 'Eliot's poetry is the poetry of breakdown.' Discuss.

(16) 'Eliot's technique brings together various illustrations of the same object or emotion.' Discuss the application of this 'assemblage' technique to any one or more of Eliot's poems.

(17) What, on the evidence of the poems you have read, does Eliot diagnose as the chief needs and major deficiencies of Western civilisation?

(18) 'These fragments I have shored against my ruins.' Discuss Eliot's use of 'fragments' in composing his poetry.

(19) 'Eliot's obscurity is not as remarkable as his clarity: his vision is as clear and exact as the language by which it is communicated.' Discuss.

(20) In what ways do Eliot's critical opinions throw light on his poetic practice?

# Writing an essay

After you have made notes on some of the above topics, you may want to tackle essays on them. There are a few further points to bear in mind when writing essays, whether against the clock or not.

Write about the chosen or set topic and about that only. If you are answering a question about the nature of Eliot's imagery in 'Marina', do not get sidetracked into a discussion of the state of English poetry in the 1920s, just get started with some such words as 'The imagery in "Marina" is . . .'

Before you start writing, however, you should plan your essay. Jot down ideas, then arrange these under headings (which will form the paragraphs of the essay), noting suitable examples from the poems under each heading. When a methodical plan is clearly thought out in advance like this, it is much easier to set about writing in an orderly way. Write as simply and clearly as you can. At the same time try to avoid dullness by varying your sentences and, if possible, sounding interested in what you are doing.

# Specimen essay plans

In many essays you can choose either a chronological approach or a thematic approach. For the first, go through a poem or selection of poems from start to finish, or early to late; what you discuss and the order in which you discuss it is determined by what you find in the poetry as it is arranged 'in time'. For the second, follow up certain themes, points or ideas, calling on different parts of a poem or poems as you turn to each new heading. Sometimes you can combine these two approaches. The chronological essay scheme takes the form of 'First he does this, then this, and finally this'. The thematic essay scheme takes the form of 'First let us look at theme X, as illustrated in examples A and B; then let us turn to theme Y . . .'. A combination scheme has wider possibilities of variation, but may take some such form as looking at early examples of themes and then later examples of the same or other themes.

Here is an example of a chronological scheme for a general analysis of 'Portrait of a Lady':

|  |  |
|---|---|
| (*i*) FIRST VISIT: | December scene—fog |
|  | Affected setting and speech |
|  | Music (to tom-tom) |
|  | Friendship |
|  | Escape |
| (*ii*) SECOND VISIT: | April scene—lilacs and longing |
|  | Music returns |
|  | Appeals repeat |
|  | Escape—but music and hyacinths |
| (*iii*) THIRD VISIT: | October scene—stairs |
|  | Abroad |
|  | Friendship again |
|  | Pretence |
|  | Escape |
|  | Doubts—final music |

Here is an example of a thematic scheme for a general analysis:

| | |
|---|---|
| (*i*) STRUCTURE: | Monologue |
| | Three visits (present tense) |
| | Conclusion (future tense) |
| (*ii*) VERSE MOVEMENT: | Rhymes |
| | Rhythms |
| | Regularity versus irregularity |
| | Repetition |
| (*iii*) THEMES: | Her frustrated life, longings |
| | His shrinking from life, rejection |
| | His and her affectations |
| | Her genuine values, his sincere doubts |
| (*iv*) IMAGERY: | Scene—seasonal images |
| | Her affectations—setting and speech |
| | His reactions—satire (Juliet, Chopin, 'musical' conversation, tom-tom prelude . . .) |
| | Her longings—spring (lilacs, sunsets, Paris, buried life . . .) |
| | His shrinking and guilt—smiles, escapes, faltering (flame), doubt (piano, hyacinths, her music) |
| | Entrapment—tomb, tea serving . . . |
| (*v*) TONE: | Narrator's attitude to Lady—superior irony |
| | Narrator's attitude to himself—self-deprecatory irony |
| | Changes of tone |

Here is an example of a thematic scheme for a question on the imagery, partly using the chronology provided by the three sections of the poem:

| | |
|---|---|
| (*i*) MUSICAL MOTIFS: | (*a*) Chopin satire |
| | Violin and cornets match speech |
| | Tom-tom headache |
| | (*b*) Violin and voice return |
| | Street piano—memories |
| | (*c*) Dancing bear—to her tune |
| | Her 'music' successful |
| (*ii*) SEASONAL IMAGERY: | (*a*) December smoke and fog |
| | (*b*) April lilacs, sunsets—longing, buried life |
| | August memory |
| | Back to spring—hyacinths |
| | (*c*) October darkness |
| | Mixed time of death |

(*iii*) SOME OTHER IMAGES: Candles—Juliet's tomb; self-possession
Trapped indoors—tomb, tea, clutter, stair, repetition, captive animals
Outdoor escape—air, cigarettes, drinks, park

When writing an essay, whatever type of plan you follow, remember it is usually best to get straight to the point and launch into your first paragraph (from the first heading) without any padded-out introduction. Similarly, there is often no need for a concluding summary of the previous points. When you have said what you have to say, stop—and perhaps•try to give the last point in your last paragraph a fitting concluding emphasis.

---

### Specimen essay 1

---

For instance, you might have turned the last scheme into an essay of about a thousand words that went something like this:

The images in 'Portrait of a Lady' that immediately strike the reader are the musical ones, which appear in each of the three parts of the poem. These musical motifs help to link the sections and, by recalling previous uses of music in the poem, can be used to evoke and comment on moods and memories that have previously been established. Perhaps this is one reason why the first section (which has to do the establishing) contains more examples of musical images than the other two sections —with more repetitions, just as in the repeated phrases of ordinary music—as if to prepare the reader for a 'musical' use of words, letting the technique of repetition with variation add its effects to the evolving sequence.

As with most of the imagery in this poem, the musical images are used initially in a satirical way; it is only later that ambivalent emotions creep in. The piano-playing of 'the latest Pole', transmitting Chopin through his hair as well as his fingers, suggests an affectedly 'spiritual' artistic sensitivity matching that of the 'lady' herself, as she gushes into speech about the composer's 'soul' and his 'bloom', as of a delicate exotic fruit, which is rubbed off by the common public at concerts. This paralleling of music and affectation continues with the explicit linking of the rarefied genteel conversation with the gentle music of ethereal violins and distant cornets—humorously underlined by the pun on 'composed' to describe the lady's life. This first section ends with a reappearance of the violins and cornets, 'winding' or performing elegant 'ariettes' in a way that echoes the lady's elegant repetitiveness— which in turn starts his own one-note 'tom-tom' prelude beating in the young narrator's brain, 'one definite "false note"' to give him a headache and make him long to escape. In the second part, however, repeated instances of music do not only irritate the young man ('the insistent out-of-tune/Of a broken violin'; 'a street piano, mechanical and tired / Reiterates some worn-out common song'); they also demonstrate the power of the most undistinguished music to evoke memories, to invest commonplace recollections with a new strength of feeling; and therefore, as unhappy reminders, to make him lose his self-possession and experience his first doubts. This takes us through to the third section where, though he remembers having to dance to the lady's tune like some trained bear, it is her higher feelings that still pursue him; her 'music' still triumphantly sounds in his mind's ear, for all the affected melancholy shown by the Shakespearean 'dying fall'.

Whereas the musical images help to unite the parts of the poem, Eliot's seasonal imagery distinguishes the different times of year in which the different events of the poem occur. Darkness characterises the late months of the outer sections; sun and flowers characterise the middle section. So the initial 'smoke and fog of a December afternoon' of the first visit to the lady is set against the central April sunsets and lilacs, spring images of the lady's longings and her revived memories of the youthful past of 'My buried life, and Paris in the Spring'. During this spring visit, however, the lady's irritating speech reminds the young man of an irritating violin heard in the heat of high summer; and it is not until he has escaped that the smell of more spring flowers (hyacinths) combine with music to make him think of the desires of people like the lady, and wonder if his critical attitude is the right one. The third visit finds darkness again in the descending October night, but when the narrator thinks of the lady's future death, it seems as if her spring sunsets ('yellow and rose') alleviate the 'grey and smoky' afternoon of her imagined day of death—another victory for the lady?

Other uses of imagery in 'Portrait of a Lady' include the candle images, in the four candles to indicate and mock the lady's exquisite sensibility and enhance the 'atmosphere of Juliet's tomb' as well as in the candle-flame metaphors used to present the young man's self-possession as it 'flares up' and then 'gutters'. But the most notable remaining images are those of entrapment and the resulting wish to escape, which is a central concern of the poem. Both the lady and the narrator she wishes to make her 'friend' are imprisoned in different ways and are looking for a means of breaking out. The lady's drawing-room, described as a tomb, is a place where she endlessly serves tea, surrounded by the claustrophobic clutter of her bric-à-brac. It is little wonder that the young man feels uneasy about returning, and that to climb the stairs to this imprisoning room is seen as a penitential activity ('as if I had mounted on my hands and knees'): at the top he will be ensnared by feelings of guilt, at the least. The prison atmosphere is made more constricting by the many repetitions—the tea, the smiles, the lady's dozen uses of 'friend'—and is finally focused on the images of the captive animals, the dancing bear, the crying parrot and the chattering ape, used as a grotesque comment on the lady's high culture that the young man feels bound to imitate. He wants to escape from this stifling indoor atmosphere to outdoor freedom from the clutching intimacies of the lady. There the complementary images are of air ('Let us take the air') and the 'tobacco trance' of soothing cigarettes, together with a drink of beer rather than tea.

It is in the park, however, that the narrator most freely presents an image of himself as both ridiculous and sad; and it is here that we first realise he is tied down as much by his own view of himself as by the demands put upon him by the lady. Out in the park he is just as trapped inside himself as when aping her ways and bearing with her emotional appeals in the drawing-room. The painter of this portrait turns out to be weighed down by heavier chains than even its subject. Both are victims of a paralysing way of life, but at the end of the poem she will still have the whip-hand over him—in his own mind.

## Specimen essay 2

On the other hand, if you were pushed for time and wanted a shorter essay—say for a brief examination answer on the themes of the poem— you might have used part of the second scheme to write something on these lines:

The themes of 'Portrait of a Lady' apply at least as much to the young man who narrates the poem as to its ostensible subject. Both are victims of their different feelings, which hold them prisoner in different ways. This is essentially a poem about trapped, frustrated lives. It is there in such details as the captive animals (bear, parrot and ape) to which the narrator compares himself and the endless tea-serving that marks out the days of the 'lady'. This does not mean they are viewed only in a tragic light: on the contrary, they are also exposed to some withering humour on Eliot's part. This dual aspect, which is reflected throughout in the themes these lives embody—of entrapment versus escape, of affectation versus genuine values, of shrinking from life versus trying to face up to its demands, of self-assurance and superiority versus self-doubt and guilt—makes each of them tragi-comic.

The lady can be seen as tragic when we as readers begin to realise her deep emotional needs by the middle of the poem, where (a figure of frustrated sexuality) she sits twisting the lilacs and recalling her youth in an eloquent appeal for friendship. However, before this we have been made to laugh at her affectations, especially her ludicrous speech, with its soulful delicacies and 'carefully caught regrets' and exaggerated repetitions, but also such details as the 'four wax candles in the dark-ened room' that set the scene for this elderly Juliet's encounter with her latest young man.

This young man also presents himself, through the narration the poet gives him, in a way that shows him in different lights. While his critical attitude to the lady (underlined by a satirical use of music that can juxtapose, say, Chopin preludes and a drumming headache) lays him open to criticism for implied superiority and even callousness, he does give us—again in the central section—a picture of himself that is a comically-observed piece of self-mockery, also showing us he is sensi-tive, and a victim—trapped by his own view of himself. Though he has affected an attitude of amused condescension to the lady, doubts begin to enter his mind as to whether his ideas are 'right or wrong'; feelings of guilt begin to assail his stronghold. This is well caught in his frequent smiles, which may be patronising, disarming, self-assured, or pained as he tries to respond to the lady's repeated demands for his 'friendship' to brighten her nightmare existence, but which come to an end with his wondering what 'right' he has to smile at her in the first place. He is per-haps a more tragic figure than she is after all: for he is a timid shrinker from life, one who needs to escape from feeling into trivial routine, whereas the lady, for all her pretentiousness, does at least have her strongly-felt needs and values.

All the same, as the lady seems to triumph with her successful 'music' of high culture and true feeling, so the young man has developed into awareness, not only of the lady's 'advantage' over him, but also of him-self. This self-awareness makes him ultimately the main subject of the poem, the evolving of this self-knowledge its main theme.

# Part 5

# Suggestions for further reading

## The text

T.S. ELIOT: *Selected Poems*, Faber & Faber, London, 1954 (available in paperback since 1961). This is the edition used in these Notes.

## Other works by T.S. Eliot

For most other poems by Eliot, and his five plays (not including *The Rock*), see the *Complete Poems and Plays of T.S. Eliot*, Faber & Faber, London, 1969. For Eliot's critical writings, there are two useful one-volume collections: *Selected Essays*, Faber & Faber, London, 1951; and *Selected Prose of T.S. Eliot*, edited by Frank Kermode, Faber & Faber, London, 1975. The latter has a helpful introduction and notes.

## Biographies

As Eliot requested that no biography should be written, it will probably be some years before an authoritative account of his life becomes available. In the meantime, biographical information can be found in such accounts as:

HERBERT HOWARTH: *Notes on Some Figures Behind T.S. Eliot*, Chatto & Windus, London, 1965. This gives detail on Eliot's family background and education.

W.T. LEVY AND V. SCHERLE: *Affectionately, T.S. Eliot*, Dent, London, 1969.

ROBERT SENCOURT: *T.S. Eliot: A Memoir*, Garnstone Presss, London, 1971. This is not free from errors.

T.S. MATTHEWS: *Great Tom*, Weidenfeld & Nicolson, London, 1974.

LYNDALL GORDON: *Eliot's Early Years*, Oxford University Press, Oxford and New York, 1977. This is much the best so far.

## Critical works

Two excellent short introductions to Eliot are:

M.C. BRADBROOK: *T.S. Eliot*, Longman, London, 1965.

NORTHROP FRYE: *T.S. Eliot*, Oliver & Boyd, Edinburgh and London, 1963.

Longer general accounts include:

BERNARD BERGONZI: *T.S. Eliot* (second edition), Macmillan, London, 1978.

HELEN GARDNER: *The Art of T.S. Eliot*, Cresset Press, London, 1949; later printings published by Faber & Faber, London.

HUGH KENNER: *The Invisible Poet: T.S. Eliot*, W.H. Allen, London, 1960; paperback, Methuen, London, 1965.

F.O. MATTHIESSEN: *The Achievement of T.S. Eliot*, enlarged by C.L. Barber, Oxford University Presss, New York and London, 1958.

A.D. MOODY: *Thomas Stearns Eliot, Poet*, Cambridge University Press, Cambridge, 1979.

Of several symposia on various aspects of Eliot, the most easily found is *T.S. Eliot: The Man and His Work*, edited by Allen Tate, Chatto & Windus, London, 1967; paperback, Penguin Books, Harmondsworth, 1971.

For detailed treatments of sources and meanings:

GROVER SMITH: *T.S. Eliot's Poetry and Plays*, revised edition, University of Chicago Press, Chicago and London, 1974. The most exhaustive treatment.

B.C. SOUTHAM: *A Student's Guide to the Selected Poems of T.S. Eliot*, revised edition, Faber & Faber, London, 1974. The most handy treatment.

GEORGE WILLIAMSON: *A Reader's Guide to T.S. Eliot*, enlarged edition, Thames and Hudson, London, 1967.

Books not about Eliot only, but containing pioneering chapters on him, are:

F.R. LEAVIS: *New Bearings in English Poetry* (second edition), Chatto & Windus, London, 1950; paperback, Penguin Books, Harmondsworth, 1963 and later printings.

EDMUND WILSON: *Axel's Castle*, Charles Scribner's Sons, New York, 1931; paperback by Fontana, London, 1961.

# The author of these notes

MICHAEL HERBERT was educated at the Universities of London and Oxford before taking up a lectureship in English at the University of St Andrews, where he specialises in English literature of the twentieth century. He has published critical works on various modern writers, and is currently working on a study of D.H. Lawrence.